TRAVELS IN ITALY
From Verona to Roma

David D. Hume

PublishingWorks, Inc.

Exeter, NH

2009

PublishingWorks, Inc.,
151 Epping Road
Exeter, NH 03833
603-778-9883

For Sales and Orders:
PublishingWorks, Inc.
60 Winter Street
Exeter, NH 03833
1-800-738-6603 or fax 603-772-1980

Designed by Kat Mack
Edited by Melissa Hayes
Front cover art: Virginia Wright-Frierson

LCCN: 2008925467
ISBN: 978-1-933002-78-1

TRAVELS IN ITALY

From Verona to Roma

In memory of Sigmund Diamond,
who first taught us about Rome.

Also by David D. Hume:

Nonfiction:
Blueberry: A Boat of the Connecticut Shoreline
About Italy: Puglia to the Po
About Sicily,: Travellers in an Ancient Island

Fiction:
Beyond the Long-Eared Mountains

TABLE OF CONTENTS

GERMANY

SWITZERLAND   AUSTRIA

FRANCE   DOLOMITES

ALPS   *Bergamo* •*Trento*   SLOVENIA
                      Vicenza *Treviso*
        Milan *Verona* *Padua* •*Venice*
  Pavia• •*Piacenza*
  Turin   *Mirandola*   CROATIA
  Genoa *Parma*
        •*Chiavari*   ADRIATIC
              APENNINES **Bologna**   SEA
          Lucca• *Forlì*
              Pisa   BOSNIA-
  LIGURIAN SEA   *Rimini*   HERZEGOVINA
              Florence *Urbino*
                      Perugia
              Siena
              Viterbo *Ascoli Piceno*
  CORSICA   *Rodi*
              Orvieto APENNINES *Garganico*
              Rome
                          Trani
                                  Ostuni•
  SARDINIA   *Naples*   *Lecce*•
                      Paestum

        TYRRHENIAN
            SEA
                                  IONIAN
                                    SEA
                      Palermo
                          Mt. Etna
                      SICILY
                          Syracuse

ITALY

Hale

AUTHOR'S NOTE

This series of essays of travels in Italy is a revised and augmented version of my earlier book, *Towns of the Renaissance*, first published in 1998. This edition includes a number of drawings from that book, as well as newer illustrations by my friend and collaborator, Mary Elizabeth Miner. The cover design is from a painting by Virginia Wright-Frierson. There is a great deal of new material on Rome and Florence.

My thanks to Jeremy Townsend for providing much good advice while urging me on with great patience, and to Melissa Hayes for assembling the text from previous fragments and new overlapping versions of our adventures in Italia.

Most of all, Cathy Hume, lovable critic and fellow traveler, always communicated a belief in the final product even when reading the smallest scraps of an uncertain design.

DDH
Wilmington, North Carolina
Salem, Connecticut

Preface

When we first saw it, the little brown building didn't look very promising as we approached after paying for tickets in the small museum shop. There was some pipe scaffolding and plastic tarpaulin drapery over one end. We entered through a low door and blinked momentarily in the dimly lit room.

And then we saw them. Huge panels of painted figures on the walls, huge paintings, dozens and dozens of them in reds and blues, in buff, ochre, and umber modeling. Row above row of great frescoed panels showing landscapes and cities, shepherds, donkeys, angels, Magi, Pharisees, sinners, bystanders, and penitents, covering the entire walls of the Scrovegni Chapel with a complete Last Judgment over the entrance door. The colors are so rich, the figures so human, the story of the coming of Christ, his life and death so explicit, so overwhelming, so persuasive that we realized this was why we had come to Italy in the first place, to Padua, to be enveloped in this middle-sized room that Giotto had transformed into a place of assent and of worship in the first few years after 1300. In the process he also transformed European art and started what we now recognize as the Renaissance.

Anyone whose subconscious mind was cultivated in youth by the plowshares and swords of a liberal education must have thought about a trip to Italy at some time or other. Those furrows dug in the psyche by the experience of classical art and history are pretty much permanent. We still remember, perhaps, a few lines from "Horatius at the Bridge," and something of the glory that was Rome when it was the center of all the world. We still wonder at the causes of the gradually accelerating disaster of its decline in the third and fourth centuries, or of the long, confused dark and savage time when the "Eternal City" shrank to become a town smaller than New Milford, Connecticut; smaller than 15,000 more or less miserable people patching up their houses from the broken pieces of the palaces and temples that once surrounded the Forum. We may remember the beginnings of something more vigorous emerging from the fierce carnage of the discord among the new warlords, of bloody conflicts and mutual exiling of Guelphs and Ghibellines, of private wars and rapacious popes. Then came something better—the delight of a new poetry, a renewal of old learning, the growing civilization of the successful warriors, a rediscovery of the forms of classical design and figure modeling: the Renaissance. It seems to have dawned in the early fourteenth century and lit up southern and central Europe for the next two hundred and fifty years. In many ways it never stopped. New learning emerged from the old, and the scientific and industrial revolutions flowed naturally from its beginnings to the achievements of the inquiring and avaricious minds of the modern Europeans.

Most of these currents of thought and inventions became evident in the late fourteenth and early fifteenth centuries. Things that happened in banking, astronomy, anatomy, architecture, representational drawing, commerce, and law started in the centuries that came a thousand years after the first barbarian sack of Rome. A little less than a thousand years after Constantine moved the center of world power to the East, Giotto began painting the walls of the Scrovegni Chapel with human figures that left the chunky

Romanesque and attenuated Gothic forms forever behind. In the explosion of exploration, religious reformation, artistic innovation, and architectural engineering that followed, the old world of the Middle Ages was transmuted into the modern world. However held in loyalty to the church it may have been, the intellectual, artistic, and architectural foundation of most of what happened in that amazing time took place in a handful of northern Italian cities, although not in Rome itself.

Although Italy may be politically inept, economically unstable, Mafia-bedeviled, or blinded by sentiment and uncontrolled passion, it is still the birth location of much of our intellectual ancestry, and we must experience it. Besides, it is beautiful, often has agreeable weather, and the food, which was deplored by eighteenth-century English travelers, is wonderful today. Those peripatetic Brits had probably been brought up on boiled beef and horseradish.

When my wife and I undertook our first Italian trip, we were in our sixties and very much able to walk briskly for good distances. We were of an age when "sensible" shoes look appropriate by day and a woman can get by with only one other pair of footwear in her luggage. We decided to go on our own and do without the preplanned itineraries and guided group tours offered as packages by undeniably helpful travel agencies or by the fund-raising offices of our college alumni associations. We stayed at modest hotels, ate mostly in simple restaurants, and moved about the country on short-haul local trains. On several trips we availed ourselves of the smallest rental car we could charter. We got a lot of Italy for our money, and we made closer contact with both city and country than tour guides could have arranged for us. In this book we hope to encourage others to do the same.

Tuscany in spring.

I

FROM MILANO TO CREMONA
Starting in a Small City

We sometimes took Alitalia to Milan and would like to do so again. Their transatlantic planes have often been comfortable 747s with seats pitched to give a little extra leg room; the food is excellent, departure and arrival schedules are convenient, and the nice, bilingual cabin attendants got us accustomed to some clearly enunciated Italian before we were faced with the immediate necessity of distinguishing hot and cold from *caldo e freddo*. Rome requires more of a knack for Italian travel.

When you arrive in Italy, you will need to have some money. Large American banks at home can buy you some euro at a not-too-terrible exchange rate. Bring a couple of hundred dollars' worth of euro when you come and then get more on a Visa or AmEx card at a Bancomat (an Italian ATM). Banco National di Lavoro and the Banco di Roma have lots of branches with such cash machines that will give you 300 euros at a clip. In trying to figure out how much things cost in home currency, we got used to thinking in terms of the worth of the euro—a little less frightening than thinking of the rate of the sagging dollar! The public *cambio*, traveler's checks, or even trading dollars at a bank window will produce a worse rate of exchange. Visa or AmEx debit cards are the best deal, giving you the wholesale rate of exchange. Credit cards do charge you interest for a couple of weeks' use of the money.

Milan is a better place to get started than Rome. If the northern city is a little busy and commercial, we have found several reasonable hotels in the vicinity of the duomo. But even better, there are places like Cremona and Verona within a two-hour train or automobile trip. Once we got a car at Malpensa Aeroporto and drove to Como by the lovely lake to sleep off our jet lag in style at the Hotel Metropole et Suisse. But since we usually arrive in Italy at 9:30 in the morning, there was also plenty of time to take the bus in to the Stazione Centrale of the state railroad in Milan and get one of the frequent trains to Verona or to Cremona. Either trip takes an hour and a half and you can be settled into your hotel in time for an afternoon nap and some recovery from the disorienting shift of living in a world six hours ahead of time. If you need lunch while under way, many trains have bar cars or full-sized diners. There is a large poster board on every railroad platform with symbols showing the makeup of each train, including such facilities. Cars are labeled with numbers 1 or 2 to indicate class. Second class is just as swift, clean, and civilized as the best to be found on Amtrak, even if the seats are a little less luxurious. Fares are modest, and we saved money by *not* using the various rail passes offered to tourists. Most of these are discounts off first-class bookings. You have to do a powerful lot of long-range travel to profit much from them. For short hops around the north, ordinary second-class rail tickets are quite cheap. (At the moment you can go from Firenze to Roma for approximately $70.)

All things being equal, we would perhaps recommend Cremona for a first night in Italy. In the pattern of seeking inexpensive lodging, we put up in Cremona at the Astoria, a pleasant little hotel in a splendidly central location and equipped with a nice little lobby bar for cocktails or breakfast, for about 120 U.S. dollars. We were a minute's walk from the piazza that fronts on the cathedral, the campanile, and the Palazzo Comunale. That building is a remodeled thirteenth-century palace which has a sumptuous display room upstairs that contains four of the world's most famous violins, now the property of the town, although played from time to time by visiting musicians. They are examples of the greatest of the Cremonese violin makers: two Amati, one Guarnerius, and one Stradivarius. The great stairway to the violin room is more easily walked down than up. It is a magnificent piece of architecture, but it is nice that there is now a lift to get to the top.

Cremona has a pleasant little park in the midst of things, featuring the tomb of Antonio Stradivari and (at some distance) a life-scale sculpture of three husky girls who may be intended to represent a modern version of the Three Graces. In any case, they are built like true *contadine*, sturdy of breast, belly, and buttocks, giving a good example of the obvious truth that the great Renaissance sculptors were not "realists" in any sense of the word. The girls who modeled ideal beauty for them couldn't have evolved to be *that* different in five hundred years without the aid of genetic engineering. The idea of a mid-city park is unusual in Italy. This one marks the site of a Dominican monastery that was torn down in a brief fit of anticlericalism during the *Risorgimento* in the nineteenth century.

The Cremonese cathedral, known, as are all such in Italy, as *il Duomo* (whether or not it is graced with a dome), is an extraordinary piece of Lombardy-Romanesque design that grew into the Gothic Age during the three centuries it took to complete. Its campanile, il Torrazzo, is a 330-foot wonder which is reputed to be the tallest in Italy with a wonderful view from the top. But a 110-meter stairway is one of the things that is really beyond the scope of such senior-age travelers as we. The great Piazza of Cremona is a superb example of the public squares of the towns all around the Po valley. Usually they have a cathedral, a baptistery, a campanile, and a palazzo pubblico, but in detail and sense of place, each is unique to its city. In their close vicinity are the best shops and restaurants in town. By the time we had patrolled the square in Cremona, we were in need of the latter.

Italian restaurants open late but also close earlier than most American ones. They are used to preparing for a single sitting, usually between 8:00 and 9:00 in the evening. A reservation makes everyone feel respected even when it isn't absolutely necessary, and is thus a good idea. At first, when we didn't think we could handle the *prenotazione* on the phone, we asked the desk clerk. He did it in great style, giving notice that his *clienti* were distinguished or even illustrious people, and that he would consider it a personal favor if the restaurant would arrange to give them a good table (all of which are pretty much equal anyway).

All *ristorante* in Italy divide the menu into the *primi piatti* of soups and pastas followed by a *secondo piatto* of meat or fish. Vegetables and salad are added ad lib to the second half. Sometimes, sensing that the *primo* was going to be a meal in itself, one of us would order a salad instead of a meat course and share it. This sort of thing might elicit a sneer from a New York City waiter but seems expected and quite within one's rights in Italy. Antipasto or a sweet on either end of the dinner is for special occasions, but the little cup of espresso can be a *dolce* in itself. They even make a very good *caffe decaffeinato,* usually called "Haag" from the trade name.

Cover and service charges are added to the restaurant *conto,* so a tip is often included in the price on the bill as a *coperto,* or cover charge. We learned that throwing in two or three euro earned us many smiling thanks and the feeling of being a big spender. *Mille grazie, Signore!* Usually we were able to get an elegant dinner for two for forty euro or less, including a half-liter of a very good *vino della casa.*

Breakfast in a neighborhood "bar" or in a hotel breakfast room holds few mysteries, although the former is generally less expensive than the latter. A *spremuta* of orange juice is freshly squeezed, while *succo* will be canned. *Caffelatte* is served as a small jug of very black coffee alongside a much larger jug of very hot milk. We thought it the best thing we had ever had for breakfast. The crescent rolls usually have built-in jams (all called *marmellata*), and the plain rolls and butter are often served with honey.

Although Cremona is not one of the principal centers of art in Italy, there was plenty to keep us busy sightseeing for a day, and we could have spent longer. The cathedral is vast and the town is still the world's center of violin making. The school of lute making can be visited, although we got there too late in the day to tour it. This is one of the few towns we hurried through, a mistake in retrospect.

In Cremona, as in all the rest of Italy, one sees a bewildering number of paintings and sculpted figures. The huge majority of them have religious subject matter. There are paintings, reliefs, and statues of Mary and Jesus, Joseph and the Wise Men, Peter and Paul, Francis and Sebastian, and a host of other saints and prelates that we had never heard of. To really be able to see them, to understand what is there on the canvas or on the plaster wall or ceiling, you must try hard to cultivate something of the frame of mind of the man who made the icon in the first place. Coleridge said that in approaching a poem or a drama, we must have a "willing suspension of disbelief" in order to get near enough to behold the work of art. This means that, for the most part, we must leave our rational skepticism outside when we enter the museum or church. To really see that unrealistically oversized *Bambino* suckled by his teenaged mother, who is dressed like any wealthy duchess you might come upon seated in a country cave or stable, you must, at least for the moment, decide that the Child is the Eternal One, begotten of the Father before all the ages or time or space began.

Luca della Robbia   c. 1460

Keeping that conviction in mind may be easier for traditional high-church thinkers than for the more rationalistic among us. But I have been taught by intellectual atheists, scholarly Jews, old-fashioned freethinkers, and contemporary agnostics who could enter into that believing, often even a superstitious frame of mind while in the presence of the achievements of Italian art. Let the artist instruct you; strive to understand his language. When we see Bernini's Theresa in ecstasy, we must attempt to understand and even accept the theology of a "beatific vision" that brings that expression of sexual abandonment to her enraptured face. Seeing powerful or even cruel military men who have posed kneeling around the manger in Bethlehem, think with them about *why* they were on their knees. In the presence of the greatest works of art, it is sometimes easy to be carried along by the belief of the artist. Sometimes, such assent is almost forced upon us by the stunning achievement of the painter. The artist is usually more persuasive than the theologian.

II

VERONA
A Pink and Rosy City of the North

As much as any other town in Italy, Verona is comprehended by the senses: it is palpable, luscious, redolent. This city of 275,000 has its own flavor, feeling, color, and smell. Snuggled into the double curve of the Adige (the second largest river in Italy), it is in October both sunny and damp, pink- and rose-colored, cool, fresh with the breath of the nearby mountains, and often piquant with the smells of olive oil and baking bread, the bouquet of its grapes and the pungency of its geraniums.

I wonder what Shakespeare must have actually heard about this long-lived little city on the southern edge of the great lakes that border the Alps. He certainly never visited it, but it merits mention as the center of action in three of his plays.[1] How many Anglo-Saxons of later ages have used the extraordinary comparison that "Verona's summer hath not such a flower" for some perfect maiden they have breathlessly encountered. And, of course, some, by one authority or another, have been "from Verona banished, for practicing to steal away a lady."

---

[1] *Two Gentlemen of Verona, The Taming of the Shrew,* and *Romeo and Juliet.* Even Othello mentions a ship "put in, a Veronese," presumably having gotten to Venice by canals that connected the Adige with the Adriatic even that long ago. Their courses are still traced on modern maps.

The sixteenth-century English imagined Verona as the rearing ground of the most beautiful, lovable, and faithful young women they could ever imagine. Youth and social position only delay love a little where "younger than you, here in Verona, ladies of esteem, are made already mothers." And since Shakespeare so created Juliet, people all over Italy have enshrined the ideal teenaged girl created by an English playwright in their conscious and subconscious minds, mostly without having read a word of his masterpiece of hopeless youthful love. Out on the road to Vicenza are a pair of ruined hilltop strongholds named as the castles of Romeo and Juliet. In town there are houses shown to tourists as surely being the Montague and Capulet homes of the star-crossed lovers. I guess it is a little like looking at the Church of the Holy Sepulcher in Jerusalem and quibbling about whether or not it is the real thing or merely the focus of more than a thousand years of belief. When we saw the little courtyard of Juliet's house, we were moved to believe.

But just at the moment we were surveying it, a bus stopped outside and disgorged twenty or thirty tourists who crowded in upon us and began to examine the statue of the girl in the cortile. It is a delicate but almost severe statue, very much late-twentieth-century in style of sculpture, and the maiden is modestly robed. But the stocky and be-spectacled female tour guide challenged one of the men to pose with Juliet. He grinned broadly and stood beside the statue, putting his arm around the icon of the teenaged heroine. The effect was obscene. The small left breast of the statue was polished like brass from the crude caress of thousands of such hands. One after another all the men of the group came up to take their turns clutching the brazen breast of the defenseless maiden while having their photograph taken to record their visit to Verona. It was a sort of Tailhook grab at mythological innocence, committed with much laughter and comments, which, however unintelligible to us, being in German, seemed indecent. We turned away and left the conquest of that quarter of Verona to the barbarians from beyond the Rhine.

But most of the evening crowds of Verona were Veronese out for their *passeggiata* up the narrow but central Via Mazzini and into the Piazza delle Erbe. The streets in the *centro* at five o'clock are so crowded that we had to dodge from side to side to get into a stream of traffic going in the right direction. We had arranged to meet the brother of an American friend in a café just off the north side of the Erbe, and we were glad to duck in out of the crowd. When we emerged an hour later, they were all gone.

R. Adige at Verona

Saint Filippina was standing on her eroded pedestal in the middle of the market square; or is she the Madonna? She seems to be serenely contemplating the canvas umbrellas and tin-roofed stalls that make the market a permanent fixture of the city center. I don't know how the places in the square are allocated, but, since they are crowded in quite tightly, I have a hunch they must be inherited in some mixture of primogeniture and squatters' rights that goes back to the Middle Ages. The size of each booth is standardized and there are no empty places, so I guess it is again, like the taxi medallions, a matter of whose family has been doing business the longest.

We had a gin and tonic and a *martini dry con un po di gin inglese*. Both were garnished with lavish curls of lemon peel and served in tall pilsner glasses tastefully etched with the words GATORADE. They were perfectly delicious. The smartly dressed young people arrived in droves at five during the *passeggiata* to meet with equally attractive and well-dressed friends for tea or vermouth in a very dressed-up ambiance. The café was no bar in either the Italian or American sense, and it was certainly not the working-man's tavern or pub. It would have done well in a location across from the Carlyle in the East 70s on Madison Avenue in New York.

In Verona we stayed in one of the few single-star inns of our trip, the Locanda Catullo. This inn turned out to be located on a pleasant little alley just off the Via Mazzini behind an almost unmarked doorway. Originally a men's club, the building was designed with some pretension to grandeur. In the mid-1990s, a piano studio and a couple of boutiques were located on the first two floors. To reach the Laconda you have to climb two substantial flights of stairs (which probably explains the modest government rating as well as very low tariff).

But once having reached the *secondo piano* (as in all European buildings, the ground floor doesn't count), we emerged in a sort of *piano nobile*, a high-ceilinged loggia with paintings and mirrors as well as a rather tiny hotel desk attended most of the time by the very obliging proprietor. He provided us with a nice room with a fine shower and more than the minimum ration of towels, as well as the extra *cuscino* that my aging neck requires. As obscure as his location was, he told us many people sought him out because of a plug in *Let's Go Italy*, and that the young people who came from that source were the nicest *clienti* he could ask for. He shared this information in a conspiratorial sort of way that implied his acknowledgment of our senior-citizen status as well as his happy toleration of the young at his nice walkup *locanda*.

To secure this reservation, we had been required to post a telegraphed deposit from Ferrara because it was a busy holiday weekend. At the time we stayed there the owner took no plastic and we had to wire the money order. This transaction at a post office back in Ferrara was an education in itself. Because we were checking out of our hotel, we had no "permanent address" in Italy, and although the clerk had a rack of thirty or forty rubber stamps before her, she couldn't find one that encompassed this anomaly. She finally used about a dozen of them on five or six forms, clucking her tongue the entire time at the irregularity of it all. The money got there.

The day after our rainy entry into Verona we sought out our neighborhood bar for breakfast and then climbed the levee on the bank of the Adige to walk its inner curve to the Castelvecchio and the church of San Zeno Maggiore. The little city was newly washed clean by the rain, and, as in all Italian towns, the streets had been hand-swept of the previous day's litter. Even the planting beds around the bushes and trees appeared to have been newly raked.

The color of Verona is unique. Besides the salmon brick and orange terra-cotta it shares with the rest of the country, Verona has pink marble sidewalks. This lovely stone is local, relatively cheap a few centuries ago, and durable. But among all these reds, oranges, and browns, one comes occasionally on the ashen gray and white of Roman stonework, more of it here than in any town of such size in northern Italy. Or maybe it just seems that way because of the contrast made by the cool gray of the travertine limestone with the warm clays of the manufactured building materials.

In the very center of Verona is the greatest part of a very well-preserved Roman amphitheater. The *gradini* for seating are still intact, the full circumference of the oval is complete, and all the lower tiers of seats are ready to be occupied. The pale gray stone sets it apart from the buildings surrounding the Piazza Bra even more than the difference in scale and architecture. An uppermost tier of seats was once supported by a ring of eighty triple arcades that encircled the existing structure until all but four of the spans were shattered by successive earthquakes in 1117 and 1183. This fragile remnant of the outer shell is a reminder of how grand the original stadium must have been. Today it is the scene of a summer opera festival. Even reduced, it accommodates twenty thousand people in thrall to Verdi, Puccini, and Donizetti on summer evenings. I guess this is a good reason to visit in July, since you can almost surely get a ticket. Unfortunately, we were there in October.

Verona's ruling family in the late Middle Ages was named Scaligeri, and the tribe's first real strong man was known as *Cangrande*—more or less "Big Dog," a moniker that reminds me of a desperado in an American Western. He was known in his day as a firm ruler because of his ability and willingness to discipline a subject by bashing his head in with a stone mace swung from the back of a horse. Cangrande is present today as an immensely powerful equestrian statue perched on an unlikely concrete buttress, which helps hold together the reconstruction of the Castelvecchio that has been undertaken since a bomb blew away a considerable portion of it in the closing months of World War II. The raw poured concrete harmonizes nicely with the rough stone and brick of the old fortress, and the brutal strength of it all goes appropriately with the presence of the tough Lord of Verona of the years between 1311 and 1329.

The art collected in the Castelvecchio is very much worth a leisurely visit, and includes a lovely Nativity by Girolamo Dai Libri and a wonderful nursing Madonna (Madonna Allattante) by

Canegrande: His smiling face to the contrary, he was known in his day as a firm and perhaps brutal Ruler   c. 1320

Tintoretto. Mantegna and various Bellinis are well represented. But one of the most surprising paintings (in room 12) is an amazing St. Jerome in the Desert by Jacopo Bellini. Father and uncle of the creators of the lovely childish virgins who cradle their breathtaking bambini, the senior Bellini gives us a wonderful craggy, desert-surrounded old man in ecstatic adoration before a crucifix with the open Bible he is translating on the ground before him. Putting holy writ into the common speech was obviously no mere work of scholarship, but of inspiration as well.[2]

We left the castle and continued along the riverbank toward the great church of San Zeno. The high clouds had cleared, and looking to the north, in the direction of the Valpolicella (where the wine comes from), we could see the clean shine of new snow on the sunny mountain flanks and higher elevations. A few thousand feet are the equivalent of a month's advance of the shortening season.

Saint Zeno's church is a huge Romanesque basilica that has been rebuilt several times. An incursion of Hungarians ruined it in the year 900, and it reached its present state only in the late Middle Ages. All of the lower story is round arched, but the closing of the apse is Gothic. Doorway sculptures of the original sin and the betrayal of Judas are powerful even if Eve's feet seem absurdly large. These twelfth-century sculptures contrast with Jacopo della Quercia's later work in Bologna.

---

[2] Jerome was a great scholar who lived at the end of the hegemony of Rome. He was able to travel to the Holy Land and to Rome itself when both were part of the divided but intact Empire. He single-handedly translated the Bible from the Hebrew and Greek manuscripts available to him. But on a more personal level he seems to have been a dreadful fellow. He couldn't get along with anyone, hated company, and thought women were the primal source of sin and damnation. He lived long enough to witness Alaric's sack of Rome and the beginning of the collapse of order that followed the disaster. Jerome attributed the continuing distress of the latter age to the judgment of God on the manifold sins of his contemporaries, mostly from consorting with women. His point of view lingers on in Rome.

Il pecato originale   Maestro Nicolò
S. Zeno, Verona   c. 1080

But, once inside, the Renaissance burst upon us as it did on the people of Verona when Mantegna came from Mantua to do the great altar triptych. He finished the painting in three years, completing it in 1459. It was the first work of what we call Renaissance painting that anyone in Verona had ever seen. In its spectacular setting it could easily be the first we have ever encountered. Beneath a frieze of Roman *putti* and brilliantly colored swags of fruit and leaves, the Madonna wears a red dress and a mantle of so deep a blue as to appear almost black. She balances on her knee a truly regal baby boy whose small feet seem to rest on the tips of her fingers. The eight clearly personified saints that surround her look like the original peripatetic philosophers standing in the porches of the Agora in fifth-century Athens, only their clothing is brilliantly colored. Peter, Paul, Luke, Zeno, and the Baptist are here keeping company with Mary and the child regnant, although they seem less intent on adoration than enjoying each other's intellectual companionship in a hereafter obviously intended for sages and scholars. In subject, composition, and detail, the great triptych stands in contrast to the wonderful old building it ornaments. Smiling Saint Zeno's[3] church was introduced to the absolute best of the new world of the Renaissance by the very first painting of the style in Verona. Things could never again be the same.

We walked back toward the center of town up the Corso Cavour and entered the oldest part of the city by passing Porto Borsari, a fine Roman double gateway that was constructed in the reign of the Emperor Claudius sometime around AD 50. Well-preserved Roman gateways abound in Verona. Off the north side of the Piazza delle Erbe we came to the Piazza dei Signori, which is also known to locals as the "Dante" from the statue of the great poet that rises in its center.

Dante Alighieri spent time in Verona and in many other towns while he was in exile. He was, of course, a Florentine by birth and sentiment, as well as a scholar of Bologna, a sometime soldier, and above all, a poet. The passion of his youth was spent in distant adoration of the incomparable Beatrice, daughter of Folco Portinari. She was probably about eight and Dante only nine when he first saw her and fell in love so completely, so deeply, and so purely that she remained as the goal and guiding light of all of his life thereafter. He probably only spoke to her two or three times (some years

---

[3] There is an odd red statue of Zeno in the crypt with a great grin on his face. He is the only saint we saw with such a happy expression in all of our stay in Italy. No one seemed able to explain the cause of his mirth, but the Veronese love him for it.

after that first beatific vision) and was surely never alone with her. She died when he was twenty-five. A post-Freudian world has no trouble understanding the depth and seriousness of such affinity. Children have always had real love affairs, but this one is transmuted into the stuff of myth by the genius of the man who recorded the endurance of his youthful ardor.[4]

When he grew up, Dante joined the guild of apothecaries to avoid possible designation as a nobleman and thus be excluded from political office in the democratic commune. The interminable and bloody quarreling of Guelphs and Ghibellines, and the Guelph sub-factions of Blacks and Whites, placed him in the position of judging against his own partisans when he spent a term as a magistrate. He had served as ambassador to San Gimignano and to Rome, but his known impartiality undid him when the Blacks emerged victorious as allies of Charles of Valois, who "helped" the city settle its differences. Dante was exiled for the rest of his life in 1302 at the age of thirty-seven. Traveling as we did, we met him in cities all over northern Italy, where he lived in one court or another and where he wrote the *Comedia*. Ravenna, Forlì, Lunigiana, and Verona were honored to have him, as were for a time Treviso, Lucca, and Padua, but he never returned to Florence, whose most famous son he remains to this day.

---

[4] Modern Americans are not alone in needing a guide with the skill of a Virgil to lead them through the intricacies of the text of the great Comedy. There are shelves full of translations and all have explanatory notes. It seems to me that the most lucid and engaging of these commentaries are those of the best of all detective writers, Dorothy L. Sayers. Whether you have met her detective, Lord Peter, among the great bells of *The Nine Tailors* or encountered the author herself as Harriet Vane at Shrewsbury College in *Gaudy Night*, you should get to know this peculiar lady. The final volume of her translation of the Comedy was finished after her death by Barbara Reynolds. The whole is sprightly and intelligible. More important, her two-level annotation of each canto (by poetic theme and historic reference) is much the best and most approachable gloss of the intricate text. It is published by British Penguin in three paperback volumes and should stay in print for a while.

We took the modern lift to the top of the Torre dei Lamberti and surveyed the city, both ancient and modern. The intricate S-curve of the Adige was visible although obscured by buildings. The umbrellas in the Piazza delle Erbe market looked like a mushroom garden below. The great size of the Roman amphitheater was quite clear. While surveying the snowy mountains on the far horizon, we had been standing in the campanile next to a pair of huge old bells, and, realizing that the hour was about to strike, fled down the stairs to get out of range.

In the church of Saint Anastasia there is a wonderful fresco of Saint George and *la principessa* by Pisanello, although a certain amount of the gorgeous costuming has peeled from the wall. The painting is full of mysterious detail: huge horses, tiny hanged men, fairyland castles, wilderness and domestic scenery. I was unable to find out what it all meant, but the princess is enchanting.

When you enter Saint Anastasia, whatever your faith may be, it is worth the risk to bless yourself at the holy water font at the entrance. This great shell-like basin rests on the hump and shoulders of a deformed little man, one of two *Gobbi* that adorn the bases of the first two pillars in the nave. The face of one reminds me of the handlebar-mustached leader of the posse in an old Western; the other looks very much like Charles Laughton as Quasimodo. The hunchback squints up from under brows polished by the affectionate hands of thousands who pat his head and then dip their fingers in his font, bless themselves, and pray that their sins be forgiven. His affliction can be added to the sufferings of Christ to help supply the means of our absolution. The theological correctness is too clear not to take advantage of the proffered indulgence.

We left the duomo, the Roman theater, a half-dozen other churches, and Juliet's tomb for another day and sought out a quiet bar for a cocktail while we waited out the tumultuous *passeggiata* that was starting to surge up the Via Mazzini.

Later we ate at the Trattoria Anastasia where I braved the local fare, codfish with polenta, while Cathy was served a grilled trout. We had not yet tried the *bollito misto*, but we saw it served up from a heated cart that evening and resolved to go for it at the next opportunity. The *bollito misto* is a sort of New England "boiled dinner" in the large, usually consisting of four or five different meats and sausage, typically a round of beef, a tenderloin of pork, a capon, a leg of lamb, and a *zampone* sausage made of a number of spiced meats stuffed in a pig's trotter. Generous slices of each are served with a series of mustards and fruit condiments, the whole being most properly washed down with a bottle of Lambrusco, a dry, slightly *frizante* red wine. It is a little heavy on the protein and surely the sort of thing that would

horrify your cardiologist if he found out about it, but while you are in Emilia, at least once, work up a good appetite and don't miss the bollito.

We climbed the long flights to our *locanda* with some weariness and slept very well.

III

MILANO
To the Cultural Capital

We have started many of our Italian voyages in Milan. We had already negotiated the subway, *la metropolitana*, and were considerably less intimidated by the big city the second time we visited it. And Milan is a big city. As the train traveled through seemingly endless suburbs, we looked over a great number of backyards and walled gardens, and finally rose on a sort of elevated mole that gave us a panorama of a large, modern, slightly grubby cityscape. The Stazione Centrale FS is one of those vast Victorian sheds of semicircular riveted iron arches that spans a dozen or more tracks, open on the outboard end, and full of the exciting sounds and smells of railroad trains. The metal arches rise nearly a hundred feet overhead. It must have been even more exciting when the station was also filled with clouds of steam and antique engines puffing columns of smoke. We dismounted and looked for a baggage trolley, and finding none, we learned then and there that the modern wheeled cases with integral pullout handles are essential for senior travelers. From where we left the train to the inside of the terminal, along the asphalt platform beside the tracks was about a third-of-a-mile trek.

An old guidebook's reliable recommendation aimed us toward the Gran Duca di York,[1] symbolized by a suit of ersatz armor standing at the front door of the pleasant little hotel. We liked it, but on another occasion found the Hotel Star on the Via Bossi, only three or four blocks from the opera house, La Scala. Once again, we had missed the opera season by a week, but the Tokyo Quartet was playing a program of two of the great late Beethoven string quartets. Although it was a case of being hung for a lamb rather than a sheep, we resolved to experience the great auditorium with chamber music if we could not have *opera lirica*. All tickets are dear at La Scala, but the sure knowledge that one lives but once helped firm our resolution.

La Scala is a wonderful building, both for music and for history. Our seats were in the rearmost row of a third-tier box. Fortunately, the front seats were unoccupied and we were able to move to the front edge of the box and survey the entire house as well as the stage. The acoustics of the vast hall were perfect, even for the four small string instruments, and the audience was enthusiastic. The Milanese are famous for the generosity of their applause when the work is performed well, but also known for their cries of derision if the

---

[1] There have been many Dukes of York over the years, but the one the Italians love best was one of the Jacobite Pretenders, Henry, younger brother of Bonnie Prince Charlie who was himself Pretender to being Prince of Wales. After the dreadful defeat of his brother at Culloden, York was made a cardinal by the pope in the following year. Later he was ordained a priest, and, eventually, a bishop. He outlived both the Old and Younger Pretenders, eventually becoming the last of the Stuart line. Ever ready to stick it in the ear of a Protestant English king, the pope had the old chevalier buried in a magnificent baroque sarcophagus in Saint Peter's, under the name "Jacobus III, Rex Anglorum," thus declaring the illegitimacy of the entire line of England's Hanoverian sovereigns. Although he had made the "rightful" next in line a cardinal, the pope did little to support him: Cardinal York lacked lands and benefices to furnish his state in proper Roman style. The Stuarts had fled England with little of value except their silverware. They had some property in France, but that went in the French Revolution. Eventually York swapped the royal plate to his distant cousin George III for a pension from the British Crown sufficient to keep him in decent estate in Rome until he died. He is buried beneath his father in St. Peter's, and the German sovereigns of Britannia have reigned pretty much unchallenged ever since.

artist does not live up to their standard. It is said that dreadful things have happened to croaking bassos and superannuated sopranos. On the night we were there, the Milanese loved both the quartet and the composer.

During the intermission, we conducted ourselves in the grand manner befitting the location and acquired glasses of champagne at the third-tier lobby bar. We then discovered a series of interconnecting passageways and rooms leading to the opera museum, a wonderful attic of operatic junk blended with paintings of former divas and their tenors. There was a death mask of Verdi, an oil sketch of Toscanini, a cast of Chopin's hands (rather small and slightly crooked), as well as any number of fans, Carmen sashes, winged helmets, swords, pistols, and generous, low-cut gowns of bygone Violettas and the simpler dresses of the Mimis. While it is worth half the ticket price to browse through it, you can't get through all of it in one intermission. We resolved to be in Milan for an opera sooner or later.

Milan has a clutch of good museums, but the Pinacoteca di Brera contains the most amazing paintings. Piero della Francesca's serene, if somewhat static, *Madonna and Child with Saints* includes our old friend from Urbino, Duke Federico Montefeltro (with the nick in his nose). Caravaggio and Raphael are present, as are Titian, Tintoretto, and the best of the Flemish painters. Perhaps the most striking to me was the foot-first view of the foreshortened *Dead Christ* that Mantegna painted in his later years.

Rich though Milan's museums may be, the city's most impressive works of art are the side-by-side wonders of the duomo and the Galleria. Very much in the heart of the busy financial district, the cathedral is an enormous gingerbread wedding cake of late Gothic fancy. It was started in the fourteenth century and decorated with many more than two thousand statues which are perched on every

Dead Christ

buttress and pillar. The whole wasn't finished until nearly five hundred years of creative stone-cutting had been expended. A splendid piazza overlooks the front (the latest part), and an elevator goes to the roof where an encircling series of walkways takes you over the sloping marble slabs of the nave to the very brink of the facade. It is a wonderful chance to look at the intricacies of Gothic stonework, and affords a splendid view of the city spread out around you.

Across the street to the north is one of the main entries to the famous Galleria, another poetic fancy that stretches building materials to their maximum to encompass the architect's conceit. In this case the materials are wrought iron and glass. Arches spring from the rooftops of five-story buildings to enclose a half-dozen city blocks in a gigantic greenhouse reminiscent of the Crystal Palace. Built in the 1870s to celebrate their new king, this indoor-outdoor space is the prototype for all the shopping malls that now decorate or encumber so much of suburban America. They just did it better in Milan over a century ago. There are sidewalk cafés, bookstores, fashionable ladies' shops, banks, jewelers, and art galleries in great profusion. Many Milanese take their *passeggiata* around the cathedral square in the late afternoon, but in rain or wind they crowd into the Galleria by the thousands, continuing the arm-in-arm stroll in a kind of flying-wedge formation that makes pedestrian navigation problematic.

We took refuge in one of the larger cafés and ordered our accustomed *aperitivo*. The rain showed no sign of letting up, so we later moved over to the restaurant side and ordered our early, pre-concert supper. Chance placed us next to a Japanese couple around our age.

They spoke English pretty well but were having trouble negotiating with the waiter. I plunged in and helped. The man turned out to be a retired automobile executive who had spent four years working in Dearborn, Michigan, back in the early 1960s. Obviously he learned there what not to do to judge by the inverse success rate of the cars from Japan and Michigan in subsequent years. Our conversation attracted the attention of an Englishman at an adjoining table. He wasn't getting satisfaction from his waiter on the subject of a discolored clam (*vongolo sciupato?*) in his pasta. It is amazing how far you can get on a dozen lessons from Madame LaZonga and a few hours listening to audio recordings in the family car.

The Japanese couple were much amused with the idea that we had come from America and were about to hear Japanese musicians performing German music in an Italian opera house. I countered that it was even more curious that the quartet (whose first fiddler is a British-born American of Armenian extraction) is the "resident quartet" at Yale, not an hour's drive from our home in Connecticut.

Like many of the north Italian cities, Milan came under the successive domination of powerful families and their descendants. The Visconti held it in thrall for most of the thirteenth through the fifteenth centuries. There was a short-lived Ambrosian republic around 1450, and then the Sforzas took over, smashing self-rule but also making Milan a great center of art, architecture, and learning. Having Leonardo da Vinci around for a number of years obviously helped. He rates his own museum in Milan.

Galleria Vittorio Emanuele II · Milano · 1875

IV

TRAINS
Second Class is Fine

Throughout all of this itinerant passage-making up, down, and across the broad flat valley of the Po, we had been traveling on the Ferrovia della Stato, the state railroad known simply as the FS. We usually checked the timetable at the hotel desk. They all had one, about the size and shape of Pittsburgh's telephone directory. With a little assistance from the clerk, we learned to predict passage time, and departures for any destination up to the Brenner Pass through the Alps and even beyond.

The one universally applauded legacy of Mussolini is that he made the trains run on time, and they still do. They run frequently, go everywhere, are clean, and seem governed by their own code of manners. University students (who are often commuters from small surrounding towns) move into a car's first-class section and sprawl until either a conductor or a tourist with a necktie comes to displace them. On the *accelerati* or the *locali*, which make all the possible stops, the sections are identical anyway. The only difference I can fathom is that if no seats were left, the first-class traveler would be able to claim one in the reserved section. Since we were traveling mostly in April and October, and not during the morning rush to work, we never experienced a crowded train. Incidentally, if you look like a first-class passenger (wearing an expensive hat, for example), you are generally treated as one, not questioned if you use the first-class waiting room and so on.

All the trains are electric-powered by overhead wires along the right-of-way, but not on the sidings that connect with the yards or the secondary routes to factories. In my youth, my two brothers and I owned a set of exceptionally sturdy, heavy steel toy trains by "Buddy-L." I think they were made in England but they might have been German. The tracks were at least double the gauge of American Flyer or Lionel trains, and the freight cars of three or four types were enameled bright red. This was not an electric train: You pushed it around the iron track and onto the turntable in front of a huge three-chambered roundhouse. We had four or five pieces of rolling stock, a hopper car, gondola, flatcar, and caboose, all of which seemed quite realistic when I was eight, even though they were the European single-axle sort of wagons. But the engine was always a disappointment to me. It just didn't resemble the huge, brawny, 4-6-4 steam locomotives that I saw pulling trains through New Milford, Connecticut, in the 1930s. Buddy-L had foisted off on us a dark green vehicle that looked rather like the engine hood and cab of a semi-trailer rig set on steel wheels. Now, at last, I understood and forgave them a lifetime of doubting their integrity. The diesel-powered switching engines of all those small Italian towns were perfect replicas of the green Buddy-L engine, and most looked to be about the same age.

We have only good things to report of the FS. Schedules were clear and easy to find. Stations were manned (or often womaned) by people who knew what was going on and communicated it well even when they didn't speak English. On the one occasion that we took a *Rapido* (now known as an EC), we found that the restaurant car served us elegantly and with very good food. If it cost more than most lunches, it included a fine *linguine al funghi*, fresh fruit, and, although we ordered wine by the glass, the waiter poured it generously from a newly opened bottle of Verdicchio. For a return to the luxury now lost to our civilization and a stunning contrast with the airlines, you really should schedule a trip or two on a medium-range train with a real dining car.

On the other hand, there are some places in Italy that really require an automobile to approach. I guess there are others that require a saddled mule.

V

FERRARA

A City of Intelligent and Beautiful Women, a Few of Whom Were Very Rich and Powerful

Bologna and Venice, enormously different as they are, seem at least to be occupying the same time zone of history. Both are very cosmopolitan cities. One would feel quite unsurprised to encounter a movie star or television personality on the streets of either one. Not so in Ferrara. This town has a simplicity, almost a naiveté, about it, as though it belonged to another time and hadn't yet joined the later twentieth century, much less the twenty-first.

One of the best simple hotels we found in Italy was the Albergo San Paolo—well appointed, clean, and charging about $150 a night with shower and plenty of towels. Its location just inside the old city wall was beside an innocently empty square less than a five-minute walk from the duomo. There is a cheerful little bar next door that provides jam-filled buns and cappuccino for breakfast.

The morning after our arrival, we woke to find the quiet space in front of the *albergo* filled with panel trucks, trailers, and small-scale RVs. Poles and awnings were sprouting in various directions from the vehicles and a multitude of folding tables were being filled with merchandise. Evidently, we had hit upon the day of the weekly market. Sweaters, raincoats, foundation garments (including bras in an amazing variety of sizes), shirts, socks, tools, *gelato* in many flavors, Coca-Cola, cheese, and shoes with stiletto heels were laid out in profusion at prices set to attract the common man and woman. I found a couple of pure cotton handkerchiefs printed in paisley patterns and sporty colors—very much the thing for the breast pocket of the dark blue blazer I wore all over Italy.

Progressing into the *centro storico*, we began to hear the hesitant strains of a semiprofessional military band, mostly trumpets and drums. The bandsmen, some of them boys and girls, were gathered in the courtyard of the Palazzo Comunale. They accompanied a squadron of costumed men of mixed ages who were carrying fluttering black and white checkered flags which they waved in unison and hurled into the air to catch with a flourish as they descended. Breaking into two ranks, they took to tossing the flags back and forth over a widening space between their leaders. The band played while a largely nontouristic crowd admired their skill and applauded. After a while the musicians formed into a parade and led the populace down the street to the cathedral where they shaped up to salute a sizable contingent of people in mufti who filed into the church. Many wore colored ribbons in their lapels, and we eventually learned that the whole affair was a salute to the blood donors who were going to have Mass celebrated in their honor. It all seemed an expected and appropriate way to encourage civic virtue.

The very center of Ferrara is the castle of the Este family. Niccolo III built it and dug its moat (which is clear, being fed by a freshwater spring) to protect himself and his family after 1385, the year in which they had a close go with an uprising brought on by too stringent a tax policy. This is one of the few cases of a large chunk of military architecture being dedicated to protecting the ruler from his own people.

The Estense took a firm hand in most things. Niccolo later discovered his attractive young wife *in flagrante delictu* in the arms of his own bastard son. You can visit the dungeon where he briefly chained them up before having them beheaded. I have read that both Donizetti and Mascagni made operas based on this regrettable affair, but I have been unable to locate either in the Metropolitan Opera's reference book. Perhaps they are sung only in Europe. Browning's "My Last Duchess" attributes a similar style of family discipline to another duke of Ferrara who thought his wife responded too readily to the compliments of a monkish painter whom he had hired to do a likeness of her.

Ferrara in the fifteenth century was four times the size of Rome and the most brilliant court of Europe. A bit later, writers Torquato Tasso and Ludovico Ariosto lived here and found the intellectual climate stimulating. The real center of all Ferrara's activity was to be found in the influence of its women. Ercole I, Duke of Ferrara, had two daughters, Beatrice and Isabella d'Este. The girls were not only beautiful; they were also intellectual, educated, and possessed of the taste that set the fashions for *quattrocento* Italy as well as the rest of Europe. Beatrice eventually married the Duke of Milan, Ludovico Sforza, and Isabella married Gianfrancesco Gonzaga, the Marquis of Mantua.[1] Their

---

[1] Isabella was a spritely fifteen-year-old when she married and moved to Mantua. She wrote home to her unmarried sister to say, "I am yoked to a ducal stable boy who belches, farts and spits on my train as readily as he slobbers over my hand." Yet the marriage was a long and relatively faithful one and did honor to both. He provided financing for Giulio Romano's lovely Palazzo del Te, where his young wife and son developed one of the prettiest little palaces in the whole country. She wrote some pretty spicy stuff in letters to her sister, many of which have been preserved in the archives of the family in Ferrara. More about her in chapter 6.

There are a number of books about these fascinating ladies. At the end of the nineteenth century, Julia Cartwright wrote biographies of both Beatrice and Isabella d'Este, the latter published in London in 1902. Although the author was a Victorian bluestocking scholar, her accounts make good reading today, and provide copious quotations from Isabella's letters in sensible English translation.

brother, Alphonso I, in a stroke of political good fortune, acquired the daughter of the pope as his wife.

Lucrezia Borgia had two husbands before Alphonso Este. One died under questionable circumstances (strangling?), and the other was annulled on grounds that impotence made consummation of the marriage impossible. But even though she was being used politically by her father and her brother Cesare in all of these nuptial alliances, Lucrezia was very much a person in her own right. At the top of her form at the time of her third wedding, she was twenty-one years old, rich, famous, and possessed of long, flowing blond hair that drove most of Italy wild with delight.

When she came from Rome to Ferrara to consummate the marriage (it had first been celebrated in a ceremony with a proxy under the paternal eyes of the pope), the event provided the most spectacular procession in a century known for such ceremonies. In his gold mine of information about the Renaissance, *A Traveller in Italy*, H. V. Morton relates that it required 150 mules to carry her trousseau, and that the cavalcade included a hundred male and female attendants, clowns, jugglers, musicians, and an appropriate number of elegantly dressed men at arms. When she got to Ferrara, a throng of soldiers, ambassadors, and noblemen came out to meet her. The learned doctors of the university carried the canopy over her head. Her husband (who had never seen her) came to claim her in ceremonial armor made of scales of beaten gold. Although affection had nothing to do with his choice of bride, he delighted in his good fortune of having married her and was heartbroken when she died at the age of thirty-nine.

Most of the stories decrying Lucrezia's morals and accusing her of poisoning enemies seem to have been made up by partisans of the popes who succeeded her father and wanted to blacken the name of the Borgia family by making up history from improbable gossip.[2]

From the time she arrived as Duchess of Ferrara, there was no mention of scandal of any sort. Her husband and four children loved her and mourned her death, as did a people who held her in affectionate regard. Her name is remembered fondly in Ferrara to this day (and one does not name a restaurant after *la bella duchesa* with the blond hair if there is any substance to an old reputation that she poisoned the guests at the dinner table on a regular basis).

One of the wonderful buildings of Ferrara is the Palazzo Schifanoia, a little *delizia* or pleasure palace built and decorated to the taste of some of the early Estense during the *quattrocento*. It was designed as a place in town where a busy duke could get away from the cares of office and the dullness of government. The name means "Banish Boredom!" Appropriately enough, it is now used as the Museo Civico and houses a good collection of paintings. But the treasures of Schifanoia are really the portions of the building's original fresco decorations done by several artists under the direction of Cosimo Tura. In a room used in the intervening centuries as a storage warehouse for a tobacco merchant, painstaking removal of overplastering has uncovered the frescoes commissioned by Borso d'Este[3] to celebrate the passing of the months of the year.

Originally twelve in number, these paintings are in various states of repair, but several are in fine shape. One of the best is the representation of April, filled with allegories of spring and fertility,

---

[2] Rafael Sabatini's biography of Cesare Borgia is the principal source for my own pro-Lucrezia opinions, although a number of other modern writers come down on her side. Victor Hugo, looking for a good tale for a play, seems to have done the most to magnify the sixteenth-century slander. H. V. Morton is also strongly pro-Lucrezia.

[3] He was the illegitimate half-brother of Isabella and Beatrice's father and shared in the family's good taste in works of art.

Mars doing obeisance to Venus, young courtiers exchanging shy kisses, the Three Graces showing themselves off holding hands in a corner, and rabbits preening in the undergrowth.

"Schifanoia" c. 1470

When we had gotten to the middle of town, we found that the center of Ferrara played host to a semipermanent book fair which was in session along the south side of the cathedral. Aluminum-framed tents covered the stalls. We found reprints of engravings from Diderot's *Encyclopedie,* which illustrated all that could be known about musical instruments, as well as art books, contemporary and classical pornography, novels, and textbooks of engineering, business administration, and medicine. Across the way there was a skein of inexpensive market stalls built into the exterior wall of the cathedral, giving it a nice medieval look.

Farther up the way, in the direction of the great Estense castle, the street is lined with fashionable shops. I stopped in front of a store labeled BORSALINO. Now I had heard of Borsalino, the most fashionable hatter in Europe. I lacked a hat that I enjoyed wearing, and here in the window was a pale, oatmeal-colored Prince Rupert–style hat of alpaca tweed. So what if it was marked with a small tag indicating that it went for 90,000 lire (about $70)! I eventually reasoned that such a moment would never come again and that indiscretions committed in foreign travel are the easiest to forgive oneself for in a winter of penitence later at home.

Not twenty meters farther up the street stood a statue of the original prophet of the bonfire of the vanities: Savonarola himself, commemorated here as a sort of hometown boy and hero where he received his MA from the local university. The stern young man seems to be preaching to the modern world while gesturing in the direction of the palace where the Este princesses collected art and books and patronized poets, painters, and musicians. I got no comfort from the presence of this severe preacher who inspired the cause of democracy in Florence at the end of the *quattrocento*. His *bruciamenti della vanita* during the shrovetide carnivals of 1497 and 1498 consisted of igniting a great quantity of what he considered to be immoral books and frivolous objects (hats?) in the middle of the Piazza della Signoria. Savonarola had studied drawing in his youth in Ferrara. He probably didn't burn a lot of great art in the Florentine square, but his ideas were inflammatory enough, and attracted the spiritual attention of both Sandro Botticelli and Michelangelo.

But in the short run the Florentines really preferred the Medici magnificoes to the stern leadership of the democracy championed by the religious reformer. The pope (Alexander VI, Borgia, Lucrezia's father) tried to channel his power and energy into the church's mainstream, but the monk rejected a cardinal's hat and continued to follow only the counsel of his own fiery conscience. In the long run his rebelliousness became entwined with political conflicts surrounding the battle between the papacy and the French league of cities in the north, and Savonarola was ordered to stop preaching. He was offered absolution for submission. He took to the pulpit of the cathedral again, was subsequently imprisoned, and tortured into confessions that placed him in jeopardy of the secular

SAVONAROLA
MONUMENT
FERRARA

authorities. Eventually, after three trials and much popular noise in the street, he was (with two companions) hanged in a Florentine piazza. The bodies were burned in a bonfire of their own and the ashes cast into the cloudy waters of the Arno.

Savonarola was incorruptible and filled with the passion of a wholly uncompromised, puritanical Christian conscience. He was powerful in rebuke of the luxurious and simoniac popes, but he never rejected their authority in the later manner of Martin Luther, John Calvin, or Henry of England. He seems to have accepted his own sacrifice as a necessary example to the church of his time. He was never considered a heretic by later churchmen. The stern visage of the statue bears a very large nose and heavy jaw. The piercing gaze accuses and is still scary today.

On our way back to the Albergo San Paolo we recrossed the central square by the duomo. A one-man band was entertaining a small crowd. Along with his bass drum, cymbals, harmonica, guitar, and several other instruments, he sang most melodiously in Italian. Chatting with him after his gig was completed, we learned that he was German and also spoke excellent English. He was young and very bright, but I don't think he was making a very good living performing street music. I wonder how old the tradition of the one-man band is in Italy. It would seem to go along with other kinds of street entertainment: organ grinders, street singers, and the Commedia dell'Arte of the fifteenth and sixteenth centuries. Multidexterous musicians were probably coming here from across the Brenner Pass when Savonarola was a student.

Ferrara is one of the few Renaissance cities whose walls are still intact. I have no idea when they first were raised, but the parts standing today were being worked on and improved well into the *quinquecento*. Made of packed earth underneath, I guess, they are cased in a faded poppy-red brick of a color that only old fired clays attain in time. Some groining and string courses are detailed in limestone. About fifty feet high on the outside, they are half again as broad at the top and studded with spade-shaped projecting bastions at 200-meter intervals along their nine-kilometer circumference. Each of these nodes, which jut out over a green vale or canal, is big enough to house a softball field. There is plenty of space to drive cars around the top of the wall, with walkways bordered by poplars on both sides. The whole is a mighty and impressive siegework.

Ferrara is the bicycle capital of Italy. It is set in the middle of the flat plain of the Po (*la pianura del Po*) and the pedaling is easy. The center of the city is off limits to automobiles, and the whole population glides silently about on narrow-tired wheels. The effect gives the town an otherworldly quality that we found nowhere else. It is even quieter than Venice.

Walking up one of the sloping paths that communicate with the top of the wall, I met and passed a girl on a bicycle. Dressed in the characteristic short black skirt and a blue rain jacket, she steered skillfully with one hand and held an umbrella in the other. Her face was that of a *ragazza,* between woman and child, very familiar to me. Later, I placed it. She was the very image of one of Giovanni Bellini's young Madonnas. The model might have been her grandmother by fifteen or twenty "greats." Whatever you may think of the continuation of a gene pool that would select that particular girlish countenance through that span of time, it is of note that Renaissance writers, as well as eighteenth and twentieth-century travelers, comment on the beauty of the girls and women of Ferrara.

VI

MANTOVA
The City by the Lake

After a convincing experience with inexpensive lodgings in Verona, we were encouraged to try again in Mantua. Unfortunately, in the city of the Gonzagas we encountered the only really awful overnight accommodation we found in any town in Italy. This was the hotel of no discernible number of stars that the kindly taxi driver had warned us about. In fairness, however, I must admit that the beds were clean and the bath was well equipped with a generous, if noisily ventilated shower. But a bare foot on the terrazzo floor encountered little areas of granular *polvere*, and the top of the armoire provided enough dust to defile the brim of my new Borsalino, carelessly chucked there the night before. The room looked sort of okay, but the stairs and halls seemed to be both neglected and dilapidated. On the ground floor of the building was a restaurant that had been shut down in mid-season, with the tables still uncleared of the final night's service. Perhaps the proprietario had been ill. We survived, but it put a crimp in our enthusiasm for Mantua. Besides, as a group, the Gonzagas seem to have been one of the less likeable families of the Renaissance in Italy. We promised ourselves at the end that we would come back in the future to attend an opera or a concert in the beautiful little Teatro Accademico where Mozart graced the opening night when he was fourteen. Choosing a better *albergo*, perhaps one that has three stars in the Cadogan or Lonely Planet guidebooks, would do wonders for my opinion of the Gonzagas.

Mantua is set in a freshwater sea, but land filling has made the city less defensively isolated today than it was during the Renaissance. Although it was never large, it managed to stay independent of either of the greater powers on either side of it, Milan and Venice. The Gonzagas were more crafty than powerful. As they maintained local ascendancy for almost four hundred years, well into the eighteenth century, they entertained a good opinion of themselves. This is the sort of background that allows succeeding generations of aristocrats to acquire an increasingly exaggerated opinion of their own worthiness. While we were walking through the seemingly endless chambers of the palace known as the "apartments," I wondered what use all those rooms could have. I also became increasingly aware of the inevitability of a bloody reaction to such an unbalanced distribution of material well-being that was the norm in seventeenth-century Europe. It arrived of course, when revolution and the later "terror" broke out in France a century later. Italy was not spared. Many noble ladies were killed in particularly grisly executions before a howling mob in the time of Bonaparte.

I eventually realized that the layout of the seemingly endless succession of interconnecting rooms was based on the same principles that inspired Albert Speer's architectural designs for the Third Reich. The more rooms you pass through, the more broad stairways you climb and the more decorated corridors you traverse, so much the greater must be the exaltation and worthiness of the marquis, duke, dictator, pope, or cardinal you will be honored to find in the final room. Certainly the later Gonzagas saw themselves as entitled by

divine right to live in extravagant splendor, whatever the condition of
the peasant-class *contadini* who supported all the art and luxury. After
all, they had a bunch of cardinals in the family, and, a bit later, a saint.
He was not actually canonized until a few years after the family lost
control of the town in 1708, but for most of the seventeenth century,
everybody knew that the formal designation was only a matter of
time. Named Aloysius, he was a very young Jesuit, not yet ordained
when he died while caring for victims of a plague. He was educated,
well bred, talented, and only twenty-three years old. After his time, the
rest of the family continued to commission rococo art and enjoy the
best of things in Mantua. For better than a century their conspicuous
consumption seems to have been unrelieved by any good works that
might have bailed them out of what looks like a sure reservation for
a family suite in one of Dante's lower circles.

In fairness to the earlier Gonzagas, it should be noted that they
also hired some world-class scholars to educate their young princelings
and princesses, as well as great artists to paint their portraits. Thus
they improved the lot of their fellow man by commissioning some
classy art, even if most of it was intended to show how beautiful,
rich, and powerful they were.

As time went on and decadence progressed, the Gonzagas spent
more than they could squeeze out of their peasants. A later duke had
to raise funds by selling the entire lot of paintings collected through
the centuries to Charles I of England. After Charles was beheaded
by puritans in 1643, they made a neat catalog of all the pictures and
then sold them to the highest bidders in England. Thence, through
the happy effect of high British inheritance taxes, they have been
passed into the public domain of the great museums.

Andrea Mantegna came to Mantua from his native Padua in
1460 and was set to work decorating some of the earlier rooms of the

palace. His *Camera degli Sposi* fresco shows the Marquis Ludovico and his wife, Barbara of Brandenburg, surrounded by children and pets, uncles and aunts, one cardinal, and other lords spiritual and temporal, all standing about on the walls of a small, exquisite room. Mantegna's foreshortening and perspective (especially of the *putti* in the *trompe l'oeil* oculus painted on the ceiling) are brilliantly inventive and were greatly influential with all the artists of the later *quattrocento*. In that cool and disciplined four-wall fresco, he records the presence of no less than sixteen members of the family, as well as various equerries, masters of hounds, and mastiffs. It is one of the sights not to miss in northern Italy, even if you make a day trip to Mantua for it alone.

The person who brought the most style and intellectual color to this town was Isabella d'Este. This remarkable young princess married the Marquis Gianfrancesco Gonzaga, who is depicted as the smaller of the two little boys in the fresco. Francesco took over from his older brother Ludovico. His bride first found him to be something of a boor, but when he left her alone to govern in his place while he acted as captain general of the armies for the Signory of Venice, she turned out to be shrewd in government as well as a loyal and loving wife. Her letters are the very model of Renaissance correspondence. She was described by everyone as virtuous and wise, even though she was totally convinced that her own pleasure could be defined as the public good. She read Latin as well as Italian and knew some Greek. Her demand that Aldus Manutius print beautiful and scholarly books led to some of the greatest works of the Aldine Press. Her secretaries filed away her papers and all of her letters to her sister Beatrice and her sister-in-law, Elizabetta Gonzaga, Duchess of Urbino, as well as everybody else in Renaissance Italy: warriors, poets, painters, and popes. Five hundred years later the letters make good reading. Castiglione, Pietro Bembo, Niccolò Machiavelli, and the Bellini boys were among her correspondents. Mantegna was on her household staff; kings, popes, and princes sought her esteem. Thus, before the later decadence set in, Mantua was a court of liberal learning and good government while ruled by a woman.

Isabella d'Este   Marchesa di Mantova

Isabella's portrait was painted by most of the great artists of the late fifteenth and early sixteenth centuries. In an age before *paparazzi*, the essential public relations of government was much enhanced by copious portrait painting. Other nobles, and even the pope, would request a portrait of a powerful lady such as the Marchesa of Mantua. She was usually happy to oblige, but unfortunately, most of these paintings have disappeared or been destroyed in subsequent sieges, sacks, or bankruptcies. Only a charcoal sketch by Leonardo, a medallion by Cristoforo Romano,

and a painting in full-court dress by Titian seem to have survived.
This last, which represents her in the full bloom of her beauty, was
done when she was over sixty years old, but Titian had a youthful
portrait by Francia to work from. Like so many items of the Gonzaga
collection, Titian's painting is no longer in Italy but in Vienna. It
shows her as she wanted to be remembered.

Being an intellectual and a beauty were not Isabella's only roles.
Time and again she pawned her jewels with the bankers of Venice
to finance her husband's political and military career, and especially
in pursuit of a cardinal's hat for his brother. Once, when he asked
her to provide more of such collateral, she reminded him gently
that all of her adornments were already engaged with the bankers
of Venice except for the two or three items he had given her as
wedding presents. But, she added, if their hazard were necessary
for his welfare, she would sacrifice not only them but all of her
bejeweled costumes, even if she had to appear before him, her Lord
husband, "in my chemise."

Mantegna was old when Isabella arrived in Mantua. He died
in 1506 at the age of seventy-five, and although he seems to have
produced little under her patronage, she bargained hard for his
Roman bust of *Faustina* for her collection when the artist was old,
sick, poor, and beset by debts. She got it from him by promising to
stand as guarantor for one hundred ducats owed to his most fierce
creditor. Isabella's comments about his death in her correspondence
seem curt and perfunctory. At the time she was negotiating for a
Madonna by one of Mantegna's brothers-in-law, either Giorgio or
Giovanni Bellini, I cannot remember which. There was a plague
going on, she was pressed for money herself, and her husband was
out of town at a war. Still, it seems a pity she did not have the old
man cared for more generously.

She did, however, advance the career of Raphael's pupil, Giulio Romano. Her son Federico started the Palazzo del Te down by the lake after she bought up a good part of the old waterfront to convert into gardens and a site for the building. It is an amazing place in spite of having been inundated several times in past centuries to a depth of five or six feet, with the expected effect on the lower parts of the frescoed walls. Today the whole palazzo is a museum and houses traveling exhibits ranging from the Etruscans to the moderns and presents lectures about them. It also has amazing rooms painted with giants, collapsing worlds, and the beginnings of the baroque sensibility.

Among Isabella's most valued acquisitions was a cupid thought to be a Roman antique. It was later discovered to be the work of an almost unknown young sculptor by the name of Michelangelo Buonarroti. Self-centered and tough though she may have been, the lady had a pretty good eye for talent.

After a long day in the palaces of Mantua we sought to compensate for the roughness of our lodgings by seeking out a modestly extravagant ristorante for supper. A cheap room both deserves a good dinner and makes one affordable. We eventually located the White Griffin, where we stopped to make a *prenotazione* before returning to the sad albergo for a wash and a rest after having walked over half the town. The reservation was a nice gesture, both for us and for the house, but there weren't more than four other couples there during the evening. The head waiter spread us around nicely to give each an air of being special and the restaurant an air of being occupied. I can't remember precisely what we ordered, but I think we began with a *risotto* and went on to a brace of baby salmon. With a *Pinot Grigio* from Friuli, the repast did much to restore our good feelings about Mantua.

VII

VENEZIA
La Serenissima

Venice is the world's most famous tourist town. It is also the forerunner of all the theme parks that bring prosperity to the swamps and pampas of Florida and the deserts of Southern California. The great difference is that Venice used to be a very prosperous commercial city and is not populated by characters from cartoons, but by people. The city also has art and architecture that span better than a full millennium of human achievement. In the early sixteenth century Venice began to make the transition from being the active center of all that was new in the world to becoming the greatest museum of all that once had been. The change took place when the Turks severely restricted the trade routes of the eastern end of the Mediterranean and the Spanish and Portuguese followed Columbus, Vasco da Gama, and Magellan to tap the riches of the oriental trade from the other way around Africa, or even around the whole globe. But as Venetian mercantile trade declined, the tourist traffic started to swell, and the rich and privileged of Europe began to come to see this wonder in the water. By the eighteenth century the Venetians were still building great palazzi for the rich and the trip to the city in the lagoon was becoming the *sine qua non* of a young gentleman's educative "grand tour." By the early nineteenth century it had become the most popular travel destination in Europe, a distinction that it holds pretty much to this day. The current lack of success of EuroDisney suggests that Europeans will still choose the real thing if it is available.

We approached Venice (by train) over the two-and-a-half-mile causeway from Mestre on the mainland. In theory you can arrive by air, hire a private *motoscafo* at the Marco Polo Airport, and come directly to the landing of your hotel by water. But that is a pricey way to get across the lagoon. There are also inexpensive ATVO buses to the Piazzale Romana and a Cooperativa San Marco boat that is middle-priced and perhaps worth it because of the spectacular entry to the city. It lands you by water at the very brink of the Piazzetta, right by the Doge's Palace. From there you can get a *vaporetto* (sort of a bus on the water) to any place you want to go. If you arrive by train, you stay to the end of the line, the Santa Lucia station. Outside the grand facade we came to the *imbarcadero*, where we found the *pontile* (floating dock) of the *vaporetti* that took us down the canal on one of the finest introductory tours of any city in the world. Large and small palazzi line both sides of the route, and pretty soon we passed under the Rialto Bridge, the oldest of the three dry-shod crossings of the elegant canal. Small diesel-powered work boats go by in both directions with loads of groceries, blue plastic jeroboams and carboys of spring water, baskets of laundry, and the local equivalent of Dumpsters full of garbage or builders' refuse. Everything in Venice travels by water, and aside from the two parking lots at the Piazzale Romana and the Tronchetta, there are no cars at all. The peace and tranquility this engenders is hard to imagine in advance.

Individual tickets for the boats are modestly expensive, but we finally learned to get an unlimited ride ticket for a seventy-two hour period, which was a much better deal for the four or five rides a day we took. You are never more than a five-minute walk from a *vaporetto* stop anywhere in Venice, and bopping around town by boat is easy on the feet. No one seems to check for tickets very often on the boats, but it is very expensive if are you are caught on board without one. The fine is something like €25—about the retail price of a bottle of good champagne, which I would rather have.

Venice is a wonderful town to get lost in, and you always find yourself sooner or later. There are little yellow signs with arrows and neat black lettering on the sides of buildings in some places, but there are gaps in such routes. Trying to get back to the Accademia Bridge or the Piazza San Marco, as often as not we found ourselves at the end of an alley, dead-ended at the water. Not to worry; there is always another, equally picturesque way to go.

We had located an attractive miniature hotel called Agli Alboretti a few steps from the Accademia dock. We made a reservation with the charmingly accented desk clerk by telephone from the U.S.[1] Around one corner from the Alboretti is the Gallerie dell'Accademia, one of the great collections of paintings and sculpture anywhere in the world.

Venetian painting of the medieval and Gothic periods, from the *quattrocento* to the latter part of the sixteenth century, was focused

---

[1] My prediction proved true here: Hotels of two stars sometimes have English-speaking attendants at the desk; three-star hotels always do. At the rate prevailing in the autumn of 1993, their charge of 160,000 lira for bed, breakfast, and a tiny private bath worked out to about $98 for the two of us. This turned out to be the most we paid for any hotel room on that trip, but Venice is an expensive city, and I have spent as much or more at a depressing motel with a plastic fountain in the lobby among the concrete byways of Interstate 95 south of New Jersey. I'm sure the Alboretti has gone up as the dollar has declined.

on the eternal—things that govern the life and death of mankind: sin, forgiveness, salvation, and beatitude. The subjects were the saints, the Savior, and, best of all, the mother of God. In time, bits of landscapes and cities crept in, sometimes in stunning profusion, as in Carpaccio's great cycle about the legend of Saint Ursula with all her 11,000 virgin companions. His nine paintings fill a marvelous room in the Accademia.[2]

As the fortunes of the city began to change, it became less of a center of far-flung commerce and daring exploration. The town's talent for luxury and decoration surpassed its expression of hope and new conquest. Painters began to include more local color and landscape with their iconography. Even the stark apostolic subjects of her painters began to change. Minor-league saints like Rocco[3] (for plague) became more popular than the winged lion that symbolized the patron, Mark the Evangelist. Eventually paintings of the city itself became popular. At first the elegant cityscapes of Canaletto and the gorgeous paintings of *il Buccintore,* the Doge's state barge, portrayed the strength and prosperity of the Serenissima. But the prosperity of the city was running down, and the picturesque and curious became more important subjects. Both Francesco and Gianantonio Guardi painted Venice not as background but as the

---

[2] There is some debate as to the origin of the number of the young ladies who traveled with Ursula, since there is no historical record of a girls' crusade. One theory is that her feast day was recorded in the Roman *Ordo* as honoring her with eleven companions who were virgins and martyrs. The proper abbreviation for this condition is MV. Using the number, we get a designation of XI MV. Putting a little too thin a space between the third and fourth characters, and a bit too much after the M, gives the current reading of the size of the troupe. Be that as it may, I think I prefer that marvelous army of innocents that Carpaccio saw in beatitude, being drawn up to bliss by the Eternal Father.

[3] I should not denigrate San Rocco. In his *scuola,* right next door to the Church of the Frari, Jacopo Tintoretto painted a crucifixion that must contain nearly a hundred figures, stabbing, kneeling, nailing, weeping, mocking, standing in for all the rest of mankind at the horrible, inevitable, wonderful event.

ultimate subject herself, and rendered her, even in decay, as being lovely in the fading light of an autumn evening. Strings of drying laundry began to appear in the brilliant but quickly done scenes prepared for the eighteenth-century tourist trade. Stucco spalling off the brick walls and the rotting wooden barrier doors of the water gates of palazzi along the Canal Grande became symbols of the romantic city that was quietly decaying in the lagoon off the Adriatic Sea.

It is much the same today. Even though a farsighted city administration has arrested the decay at about the 1870 stage, no attempt seems to be made to clean things up to the pristine era that began to go away around 1600. If there was insufficient laundry hanging out to dry over the back canals today, I am sure a municipal clothesline office would be commissioned to re-create the romantic decline caught in Guardi's paintings: fixing the city as it had once been, forever cherished in the minds of each new generation.

One Venetian (as well as generally Italian) phenomenon that seems impervious to decay, up-to-date, clean, and well-maintained, is the public restroom as exemplified by the one at the foot of the Accademia Bridge. It is far from the only example in Venice, and is the kind of facility that would be unthinkable in the United States. There used to be a little guidebook to the best secret ladies' rooms in New York City. At the top of its list was the one appropriately in proximity to the ceramic objets d'art on the chinaware floor of Tiffany and Co. at 57th Street and Fifth Avenue. Just head straight for the Spode and then go around to the left to find it. Venice is far more egalitarian: any stroller crossing into Dorsoduro can come down from the handsome stone landing and find the essential rest stop underneath it, convenient to the outdoor café, the newspaper kiosk, and the *pontile*, where you can catch the *vaporetto* to San Marco.[4]

Although Venice can be cold, even gray in the rain, its true colors are the warmth of terracotta, Venetian yellow, crimson, and gold. You see them painted as waterline boot tops on the commercial barges, in the tunics and mantles of the Magdalena or the Madonna. In the huge Franciscan church, Santa Maria Gloriosa dei Frari, Giovanni Bellini so clothed one of his tenderest in the sacristy. Titian gave her a crimson gown for the Assumption and painted the sky gold behind her ecstatic upward-gazing face. As the lights controlled by the slot machine winked out after their counted minute, we turned back from the triptychs beside the altar and looked down the dimly lit nave. A single shaft of sunlight from a clerestory window picked out a figure standing in the north aisle. It was a girl wearing white tights and a vermillion cape. The only contemporary in that scene, she reminded me of one of Guardi's figures giving scale and historical perspective to an early eighteenth-century painting, a genre scene of Venice.

On our way back from the Frari, we came upon a floating vegetable market aboard a pair of little barges tied up in the Rio Barnaba. The dark green hulls of the boats were ornamented by piles of red and yellow bell peppers at the bow and a dozen verdant shades of lettuce, cabbage, and spinach in wooden crates along both

---

[4] In his interesting book, *The Italians*, Luigi Barzini comments on the wonderful spirit of such public conveniences as examples of the dignity with which Italians endow even the most humble situations: "... take the majestic and motherly ladies who oversee public lavatories in parks or restaurants. They graciously open doors, hand you soap and towels as if they were flowers, exchange a few courtly words, and finally accept a modest tip with a queenly nod and a smile. What better way to spend one's life, they seem to think, than amidst the shining porcelain, the roar of many waters, the perfume of such delicate soaps, in contact with such distinguished people." My wife found the same dignified attitude in the ladies' room of the third circle at La Scala in Milan.

sides of the cockpit. It was raining, and the waterborne market was shielded by a drooping green canvas awning strung over it on poles. Customers stood under black umbrellas and spoke their orders from the quayside. We had no cooking facilities or even the situation to make a salad, but the fresh produce was so compelling that we bought a couple of oranges and three pears for the sheer joy of participating in the fresh fruit.

Rio Barnaba
ƉƉH=

Near the Rio Barnaba is the house where Richard Wagner lived while he was composing *Tristan und Isolde*. Somehow I have a hard time imagining him working out the rising cadences of "die Liebestodt" on a big square, Victorian piano in a room with a coffered, polychromed ceiling and windows illuminated by the sunlight reflected from the lapping wavelets of the local canal, but that seems to be how it happened. I had always assumed a ruined castle in the Bavarian Alps with thunder and lightning playing about the mountains. So much for my view of Teutonic romanticism.

In good weather one can sit out in the Venetian sunshine or shade until late autumn. If the outdoor tables of the Quadri or Florian's in the Piazza San Marco set you up for too costly an *aperitivo*, there are other charming places to be found. We favored a little clutch of tables and umbrellas that sprouted in good weather at the south end of the Accademia Bridge, the gateway to the sestiere of Dorsoduro. It provided a good view of the open end of the Canal Grande and was a fine place for people-watching as the gondolas bore the tourists past. We had been warned of the great cost of chartering a gondola, and at first just watched the young Japanese honeymooners enjoying themselves. But later we investigated and found that rates are regulated by the city. A good excursion can be had for about €100 for an hour exploring the canals, large and small. Now, that price wouldn't have provided an hour's worth of the services of a second-rate New York or Boston psychiatrist, and with far less benefit to the spirit.

We signed on with Mauro, one of the younger gondoliers, and set out with him on his own route to show us Venice from the water. Mauro explained that the right to be a gondolier is inherited, there being a limited number of slots available (like New York City taxi medallions). Mauro's father died early, so he came into the trade young and was happy to support his widowed mother while he himself sought a wife. He obviously enjoyed his work, and like all gondoliers, was greatly skilled at maneuvering the thirty-six-foot shell with his single scull. Gondolas are built with a twist in the keel, and thus have an inherent tendency to go to the right. Sculling with the single sweep on the starboard side tends to send the boat toward the opposite side. The combination of force and form contrive to keep the vessel on a remarkably direct and steady course. Occasional steering with the dragging scull gets one around corners, some quite sharp. Gondoliers don't sing, by and large, but they do use a series of musical shouts and bellows like an automobile horn when they approach a blind corner.

All over Italy a *ristorante* is theoretically a more elaborate and expensive place than a *trattoria*. A *pizzeria* is simpler still, but will usually serve a number of things besides pizza, often a full dinner with antipasto, primo and secondo *piatti* from a limited selection. Wanting neither to fast nor gormandize, we usually chose the *trattorie* for dinner. One of the best of the touristic eateries turned out to be Alla Madonna, in a sort of blind alley of the same name just south of the Rialto Bridge on the San Paolo side. It was less leisurely dining than some, but the food was fine and the price moderate. On several other occasions we followed a somewhat more Venetian clientele, to the San Trovaso on the rio of that name about halfway between its ends, one canal west of the Accademia. Both of these places are popular, and we needed reservations during an October visit.

Every urban neighborhood in Italy has its own bar. Not entirely what the name implies to an American, these shops serve breakfast to all Italy as well as a drink for the homeward bound in the evening. I learned that if you order your *caffelatte* at the counter and eat your panini standing up, you are charged a modest price, a sort of government-regulated schedule, but you don't have forever to keep your spot belly-up to the counter. If you sit at one of the little tables, your price will go up by a factor of two. But once you have taken the table, it is yours for the morning. Most bars will provide a local newspaper, but you can bring your own *International Herald Tribune* if you want to spread out and catch up on the American stock market or the news from home. I took to settling down to writing our journal and dispatching correspondence over the *caffelatte*. Once you have hired that spot at the table, no one will hurry you. Italian coffee is the best in the world and the ritual is a very pleasant way to begin a tourist's day. It is even said that the Italian method of sending steam through the freshly ground coffee makes a brew that is less acidic and much kinder to the gastric mucosa.

There are enough museums and churches in Venice to keep one busy for months, but there are also all sorts of other things to pursue out of doors that are worth poking into as well. In the southeast portion of the great Piazza San Marco is the huge campanile that was begun in the ninth century and completed in 1513. Topped by a weathervane to give essential clues to ships leaving harbor, it stood until 1902 when it collapsed after being struck several times by lightning. It was rebuilt immediately with the modern addition of an electric lift that will bring you some hundred-plus meters to the top in seconds. On a bright morning or during one of those magic sunsets just after the storm has passed, the trip to the top is a wonderful experience. The view of the piazza below is unequaled. Even Isabella d'Este and the Duchess Elizabetta of Urbino were enchanted by it when they came to see these sights nearly 500 years ago.

Most of the north and south sides of that huge trapezoid are bounded by Jacopo Sansovino's elegant *cinquecento* facades that contain expensive shops and the cafés that the pre-air travel equivalent of the jet set made famous in the eighteenth century. The west end is bounded by a matching building that contains a couple of banks. It was actually built in the nineteenth century at the order of Napoleon who wanted to tidy things up a bit after he took over Venice and before he sold it to the Austrians. Much as I dislike Napoleon, I will admit that the closed end of the piazza is quite elegant.

But almost exactly a thousand years earlier than this adjustment to the borders trimming the area, the eastern end of the square saw the erection of the first version of the Basilica of Saint Mark. Dark, bulbous, and brooding over the piazza, it seems an almost-alien presence in the midst of the Renaissance, baroque, or even the Gothic buildings of the town. Nevertheless, it belongs quite surely; Venice is just very old.

The Huns, Goths, Vandals, and Lombards really called this city into existence in those obscure times of the fifth, sixth, and seventh centuries. The refugees who looked for safety to the isolated islands of the lagoon were at times alone, at times owned or "protected" by the Ostrogoths who ruled in Ravenna, or by the emperors of the east who ruled in Byzantium. Torcello was the first island to have a cathedral: They started building Santa Maria Assunta there in AD 639. You can still see it today if you take the *vaporetto* #14 out to the island, about a half-hour trip across the lagoon to the northeast.[5] The seventh-century architecture on Torcello looks like some found in Ravenna. The weedy ruins of the island are romantic and mysterious. Once many thousands lived there; now, only a few hundred.

The major action shifted to Cittanova (the larger islands bisected by the Canal Grande) long before the end of the first millennium. By

---

[5] The only restaurant on the nearly deserted island of Torcello, Locanda Cipriani, is reputed to be expensive, but the neighboring island (reached by the same boat) is the lace-making center of Burano, where there are a number of nice places to eat without spending a doge's ransom for a slice of pizza.

727 Venice declared itself independent of Byzantium and elected its own duke, the first doge. Charlemagne's Franks chased a later one over to the still more distant islands of Lido for a while, but the administrative center was located at the Rialto in the beginning of the ninth century and has stayed in the vicinity ever since. This was when they started to build San Marco.[6] There is little to be seen of this early cathedral now. Most of the present basilica dates from the eleventh and twelfth centuries. Its lead-covered domes look more eastern than western, but they don't seem totally Greek to me. After many hundreds of years of building and revision, the church is *sui generis*, a type that if you find imitated anywhere else on earth only reminds you of itself.

Grecian Horse, San Marco
c. 300 BC (?)

---

[6] The patron saint of the city was originally St. Theodore. Because he was a Greek, his devotion supported the implication that Venice was a dependency of Byzantium. The prosperous families and bishops of Venice were aware of the unifying principle of having one's own local patron, as well as the prestige that came from claiming an apostle as the local hero. An evangelist would be even better. St. Mark's martyred remains were in Alexandria, where, the city being firmly Muslim, nobody much wanted them anyway. So an expedition was organized and some sailors returned to the Doge's palace bearing the holy relics of the author of the earliest gospel, symbolized by the winged lion of the apocalypse and forever after the protector of the city.

Over the front portal are the four Byzantine horses brought back from the sack of Constantinople in 1204. Those out front are reproductions fit to stand the weather and modern pollution. The originals are in a gallery upstairs off the northwest balcony of the basilica, and are very worth going to see. No one is quite sure when they were made or who did them, but they are old enough to make their metalwork an amazing feat. They are also quite beautiful, fierce, proud, and in every way worthy of their reputation. Napoleon stole them away to Paris, but the Venetians eventually got them back again. The people of Venice have rejoiced in their prideful presence for three-quarters of a millennium.

San Marco is large, complex, and rich enough to merit several visits at different times of day. Don't by any means miss the fourteenth-century mosaics that Doge Dondola commissioned in the baptistery, where a spectacular Salome dances in a high-necked, scarlet, fur-trimmed dress which complements her figure. She holds the head of the Baptist on its platter above her, dancing with a sensual animation that shows through the stone tesserae so clearly you can almost see her undulate to the music.

Later, when we had gone back to Dorsoduro again, across the Canal Grande, toward the Giudecca end of the Rio di San Trovaso, we came upon a small boatyard where gondolas are hauled to have their bottoms painted and other maintenance performed. I pushed in the unlabeled door on the land side and found myself in a dimly lit shed where there was a jig for assembling a gondola, with the keel and garboards of a partially completed boat clamped in place.

The Venetians don't steam green oak to make it bendable as we would in a wooden boatyard in this country; instead, they seem to heat seasoned wood with a large propane torch and then force the sometimes slightly charred planks onto the form. It is a mercy the whole place doesn't go up in smoke during the process. I got into conversation with a boatwright in an open-doored shop on the eastern stretch of the Zattere. He was building a small *motoscafo* on the ground floor. When I showed him a wallet-sized snapshot of a boat I had built in Connecticut, he welcomed me in and took me up to the lofting floor above, where he was laying down another boat.

Boatyard on Rio Trovaso

Gondolas evidently last twenty-five to thirty years. None of the wood is reused, I was told, not even the sculptured foredeck panels. Other than the black paint, no modern preservatives are used. Being familiar with epoxy/wood construction, this seemed curiously wasteful to me until I thought more about the Venetian attitude toward decay: it is a part of life in this city. And some wood lasts quite well by itself. The greater part of the city stands on wooden pilings sunk into the mud of the lagoon. They have been there for various lengths of time, up to nearly a thousand years. Rot spores, molds, and wood-chewing worms and mollusks cannot live in the anaerobic environment of the mud. There are said to be a million pilings under the church of the Saluté, holding up that huge mass of domed stonework. As far as I can tell, none have ever been replaced, or even could be. This situation is not unique to Venice. In New York the huge granite towers of the Brooklyn Bridge rest not on bedrock, but on fifteen or twenty feet of yellow pine beams which originally were the roof of the caisson that was worked down through the mud by the first "sand hogs" who did that excavation.

But the boats do decay, and decay seems very Venetian. Fresco painting, brushing the pigment into the wet plaster, is a very permanent art form in the rest of Italy, but in Venice the humidity has caused the destruction of almost all the frescoes and, aside from mosaics, oil painting on canvas is the most reasonable shot at immortality. I noticed that the inch-and-a-half docking lines used on the *vaporetti* to snub them up short against the landing stages were of new blond Manila hemp, a kind of rope that an American yachtsman would consider too impermanent and rot-prone to be considered for his boat. They check the boats with a confusing sort of double hitch over a pair of smooth iron bitts on the rail. Is the Manila able to grip the worn metal better than nylon? Is it cheaper even if soon abraded? Or is it an old Venetian attitude that since all things decay sooner or later, one will always have to replace ropes and lines every year or so anyway.

Walking home through Dorsoduro late at night, we came through a narrow alley and discovered a photographer with a big square-view camera on a tripod studying a little *Madonnina* in a niche with a small red electric vigil light. There was a forty-watt bulb in a little iron basket above the statue. She was protected by a chicken-wire screen and the stucco around her was streaked with rust. The photographer turned out to be an Englishman who was doing a book of pictures of Venice, all taken in available light. He was obviously going to need a very long exposure to record the eighteen-inch-high rendering of Our Lady and Child. She looked as though she cared more about the people of Venice than they merited for the care they took of her. I guess that is the way it has always been.

We visited the site of another Venetian lady, Peggy Guggenheim, whose house is now a gallery of abstract art. Having lived for many years next door to the Solomon Guggenheim Museum in New York, I felt I was sort of a relative.[7] But the paintings exhibited there belonged in a Madison Avenue gallery or SoHo. Abstract Expressionism in Venice only reveals how lousy most contemporary painting is when seen alongside the great Venetian painters.

There are many things to see in Venice, and many other things that are there or have been there that cannot be seen. One of these great creations of human art, enterprise, and energy was the Aldine Press, whose mark was an anchor entwined with a dolphin. The founder, Aldo Manuzio, was a disciple of Giovanni Pico Della Mirandola, the scholar who set out to reconcile classical humanistic learning with Christian faith. Both of these men were among the

---

[7] While that museum was under construction in the 1950s, I haunted the site. Once, while watching the "great man" sketching on a stack of plans that had been piled on a temporary drawing board, he caught my eye and said, "Young man, pass me that scale." I picked up the little triangular ruler and reached across the temporary table to give it to him. Ever since I have maintained that I helped Frank Lloyd Wright design the Guggenheim Museum. I'm sorry the city fathers didn't let him do a palazzo on the Grand Canal. He could have gotten away with it, and the sense of continuous architectural history would have been grand. I guess they turned him down because the new building might have opened the way for an invasion by Gropius, Johnson, Van der Rohe, and the rest of the practitioners of the "International Style" that would have been dreadful for Venice.

futurists of their era. Aldo came to Venice in 1490, a few decades after the first printed books began circulating in Europe. He set up a printing press and began at once to set in beautiful, legible type the Greek and Roman classics and to print them in editions both accurate and sumptuous. He also brought out the near contemporary works of Petrarch, Dante, and Boccaccio. His engraver, Francesco of Bologna, invented italic type. Aldo's work became the model for scholarly publication during the succeeding centuries, and the typefaces he used are still the standards by which modern publishing proceeds. This book is set in a face used by the Aldine Press: Bembo, which was named for the humanist scholar Pietro Cardinal Bembo, a close friend of Isabella d'Este who collaborated with Manuzio. The typeface was created in the 1490s.

The Aldine Press flourished under the direction of the family for more than a century, printing 908 different works in all. Some were done at the rather imperious command of Isabella d'Este after she left Ferrara to become the Marchesa of Mantova. Perhaps the most influential of his works was the five-volume set of Aristotle in Greek brought out in 1498, the same year Vasco da Gama got to India and started shipping spices back to Europe. The coincidence of the voyage and the book gives a shorthand version of what the Renaissance was all about.

Examining the beauty of such books, it is amazing to think of the speed with which the resulting enlargement of human knowledge was accomplished, each letter set one at a time, each form broken down after the sheets of the edition were pulled from the press so that the type could be reused for subsequent pages. I could find no site in Venice marked as the location of the Aldine Press. But faked Aldine editions and good facsimiles are still available in some of the bookstores west of the Piazza San Marco where they sell souvenirs to tourists. Look for the dolphin tangled in the anchor. Some of the facsimiles are quite beautiful. Unfortunately, the real thing is today much too expensive even for museums.

festina lente

Wandering among these shops during a trip in the mid-1990s, we came upon one that sold old prints, some perhaps regrettably taken from the cannibalized remains of old illustrated books. Among them we discovered, newly matted, an eighteenth-century view of what was clearly labeled by the engraver SAINT MARK'S PLACE. It was clean save for a touch of foxing near one edge and showed the Piazza San Marco exactly as we had just seen it, awnings hung out on the afternoon side and crowded with tourists. Only the ladies were draped in longer skirts and the men gathering in conversational groups wore knee breeches and broad-brimmed hats, with cloaks swung back over their shoulders. There was no identification, but from the costuming I would date the engraving from the 1750s or thereabouts. The little picture, measuring about four by six inches, was charming. The proprietor wanted the equivalent of about $75 for it (about the charge for a night's stay at a bed-and-breakfast in Cremona). He seemed disinclined to bargain. The shop was quite obviously a very respectable one, full of beautiful and much more expensive prints. We debated and finally distilled the general principle that, when one is gathering souvenirs on an Italian expedition, it is wise to buy a few good mementos rather than something commonplace at the duty-free shop. Besides, the print added nothing to the weight of our bags and wouldn't break in transit. Today it hangs in our Connecticut library and has given back pleasures of recollection far beyond its cost.

On our last night in Venice we walked down to the Zattere
and looked out across the Giudecca Canal. A failing orange light in
the sky made dark blue silhouettes of the work boats and *vaporetti*
plying their way across the water. The elegant shape of Palladia's
San Giorgio Maggiore marked the direction out to the entrance
of the lagoon to the east. While we watched, an enormous cruise
ship, seven or eight stories high and six or seven hundred feet long,
came from the basin on our right and proceeded slowly across our
line of sight. The ship was brilliantly lit and looked ponderously
comfortable. The passengers had spent several days in Venice. We
wondered which of the great sights they had actually seen. We knew
they had surely missed being in either Bologna or Ferrara while
on their trip, and, since the ship could not climb mountains, they
would not get to Urbino either.

San Marco and
The Campanile.

VIII

VICENZA
Palladian Villas and Barns, and a Ristorante Across the Tracks

We came to Vicenza by car and thus chose the Hotel Continental, outside the *centro storico*. Equipped with a car park and convenient to the soccer stadium, which was not in use just then, it was quite within our price bracket. The lobby and restaurant were up to "commercial" standards. We were a little nonplussed, however, when we opened the shutters of our room and looked down on a lightweight motorcycle brightly burning on the side street below. It didn't seem to attract any attention, but burned for about fifteen minutes without creating the expected gas tank explosion. We took a nap and by the time we woke up a half-hour later, the remains had been removed.

The following morning we walked into town and sought out the works of Andrea Palladio, the local boy who became the most influential architect since the designer of the Parthenon. Born in 1508 with the surname di Pietro, he was renamed for Pallas Athene, the Greek goddess of wisdom, surely an appropriate designation for such an exemplar of the late Renaissance. Many of his clients were the successful *condottiere* who survived the dangerous job of working for Venice and other neighboring towns by commanding their armies. Like generals Washington and Eisenhower, a number of these professional soldiers dreamed of settling down as gentleman farmers after the last battle was won. They had money, often lots of it, but usually no title of nobility. Yet they wanted to look important in their country seats.

Palladio was their man. He designed farmhouses of a generous but not huge scale. His designs were classical, perfectly balanced, and equipped with adjoining barns and stables to encompass the animals, the garner, and the hired hands necessary to a country home. One look at a Palladian house and you know that the owner was a person of importance, taste, and substance. In the late nineteenth century, Stanford White provided the same sort of evidence of social arrival for the new American industrial barons. There are a clutch of their houses in Newport, Rhode Island, where the architect provided instant background for the newly moneyed of a later era. And, of course, White had studied the work of Palladio.

Palladio published a four-volume set of designs (*I Quattro Libri dell'Architettura*). The books were studied throughout Europe and America during the next two centuries. Famous country estates on both sides of the Atlantic, in France, Germany, and in the remains of Czarist Russia still bear the mark of the great designer's hand.

In the center of Vicenza is Palladio's first big commission, the Basilica. It is not a church but a classical shell erected around the original Gothic town hall, which the city fathers felt needed hiding in the new age. This structure required a series of openings that would let light into the arched embrasures of the older building. Palladio managed to align the irregular spacing of the old windows with those in the new facade by the use of triple openings, the central arches with columns on either side that have come to be called "Palladian windows." Today they are made by the thousands by modern window companies Peachtree, Anderson, and Marvin, to be set oddly in the gable ends of garages and over the front doors of houses all over suburban America.

But Palladio's masterpiece in Vicenza is the Teatro Olimpico, a marvelous theater that looks small but is said to seat twelve hundred. I didn't count the spaces on the curving benches but it looked smaller than that to me. The theater is quite serene and is graced by a classical fixed background scene designed by Palladio's pupil, Vincenzo Scamozzi. It was used for an opening-night performance of Sophocles' *Oedipus Rex* in 1585. The backdrop is a set of classical buildings built in perspective so that the audience looks up several streets that recede into a distant horizon of ever smaller buildings. To complete the illusion of great distance, the stage slants uphill, away from the audience. When plays were performed against this remarkable set in the sixteenth and seventeenth centuries, a cast of supernumerary dwarfs strolled in lavish costume through the upper streets of the depicted town, appearing because of their size to be

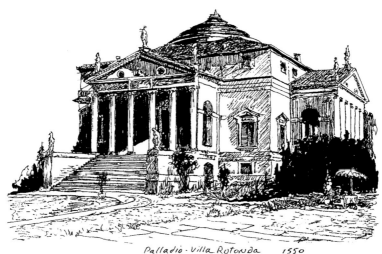

Palladio · Villa Rotonda   1550

at a great distance behind the proscenium. Once again, as in the case of the books of the Aldine Press, the masterful achievement of this earliest example of a new art form proved almost impossible to surpass in subsequent years. The Teatro Olimpico was the first roofed, indoor theater in the world.

But the real masterpieces are a few minutes outside of town. The Villa Rotonda is the origin of Jefferson's Monticello, not to mention half the state capitals and courthouses in the United States. It is a nearly perfect building, and we felt it worth the voyage just to walk around it. One of the wonderful things we discovered is that below the right flank of the formal entrance driveway is a row of arches that lead to the stables. These openings once gave passage to carts full of hay, as well as herds of cattle on their way home and manure wagons on their way back out to the fields.

Across the way is Muttoni's harmonizing Villa Valamarana, nicknamed *ai Nani*, The Dwarfs. Besides appearing in the theater as perspective lords and ladies, dwarfs seem to have been everywhere in Renaissance Europe. The Gonzagas of Mantua built dollhouses for them to live in inside their own palaces, and the royal family of Spain kept them in the household where one appears in Velasquez's great painting *Las Meniñas*. At Valamarana, their statues top the pillars at the entrance, an effect grotesque but somehow charming.

Ai Nani presents the added attraction of the two Tiepolos, Giovanni Battista and Giandomenico, father and son, as the fresco artists of the mansion and guesthouse, respectively. The painted walls of both are delightful and made us feel like spoiled eighteenth-century aristocrats by the time we had finished touring the building and looked out again on the serene valley below. On the other hand, caretakers live in the guesthouse and a homey clothesline of laundry flapped in the breeze off the perfect sixteenth-century portico.

Laundry hangs outside to dry throughout Italy, in neighborhoods both rich and poor. Italians seem reluctant to use electric dryers even when they can afford them. Electricity is almost as expensive as gasoline, and they see no need to waste it on something sun and air will do for *niente*. As a result, getting washing done by the expensive twenty-four hour laundry service that three-star hotels offer always seemed to produce shirts that were well ironed but a trifle damp when they were returned with the bill.

Feeling a little like properly entitled nobility after a day touring the wonderful villas, we were not amused to discover that the entire hotel dining room had been interdicted by the reservation of a group tour. They had arrived in their transalpine juggernaut while we were out indulging in the pleasures and amusements of their betters. The desk clerk recommended a restaurant a few blocks away and we set out in the dark to find it. After some exploration, we located the place and discovered it to be *chiuso*.[1]

At this point we met another couple walking the street in the dark. They spoke a little English and we were able to get across the idea that we were in piteous need of something to eat. They pointed us off into the night with instructions to turn left after we crossed the railroad tracks. We pressed on with great faith, through a rather desperate part of town, and were eventually rewarded by the sight of a little building with red-curtained windows that bore the rather pretentious title for so small a place of Ristorante Il Tinello. Being at the beginning of our study of Italian, we were unable to do much with either the menu or the voluble staccato of the proprietor, who

---

[1] We got used to this word, and found it prominently displayed on almost every building in Italy between 1:00 and 3:00 PM. When all the town is *chiude*, it is time to go back to the hotel and take a nap, read the guidebook, or perhaps tend to each other's affectional needs as does the rest of Italy through the midafternoon.

was finishing up service to the twelve persons of an anniversary party who were the only other patrons that late at night. I finally lurched out enough bad Italian to say that we were in *i sui manni*, or something to that effect, hoping to mean that he would have to do the ordering for us. He beamed, disappeared into the kitchen, and came back with a lovely bottle of Soave followed by a succession of antipasti, primi piatti, and eventually, a great variety of specialties that made up one of the most wonderful dinners we have ever eaten. I have only a shaky idea of how to find Il Tinello again other than through the matchbook I saved: Corso Padova 181; Tel. 0444 / 500325. If you are able to find the place and eat there, I hope you will tell the *proprietario* that you came at the behest of a lost American couple whom he treated with exemplary kindness and great culinary skill one night. Also say that the author of this book would like to return after fifteen or twenty years and let him select the dinner again.

We saw a number of fascinating and elegant buildings in and around Vicenza. One humble structure sticks in my mind and was possibly not drawn by either Scamozzi or Palladio. Turning the car around in the dead end of a muddy barnyard in the valley across from the Palladian Abbey of Monte Berico, we noticed a trio of large doorways. They led to a shed of indeterminate age that contained bales of hay, a wagon with modern automobile-style wheels, and a substantial pile of rusted junk. It was the sort of detritus filled outbuilding I have seen on an old farm near Colchester, Connecticut, except that here the lintels of the doorways were supported not by rough-hewn chestnut beams, but by graceful Roman arches and slender Doric columns done in stucco over brick, Andrea Palladio's preferred materials for domestic architecture.

IX

BOLOGNA
The Learned or the Fat

We came to this modern and very cosmopolitan city on a fast train, speeding smoothly down the Po valley in great comfort. We tried to imagine what travel or even daily life itself could have been like in this same area when the Western Empire of Rome came slowly to pieces in the years following the Visigoths' invasion. Alaric took Rome in 410. Britain saw the end of direct command of the legions from Italy in the same years. The Saxons, Angles, and Jutes started coming across the Channel soon thereafter.

In civilized Emilia-Romagna, where Bologna—with a population at that time of over 20,000—had been considered one of the most opulent small cities of the Empire, the process was slower but just as devastating. Records are missing for much of the period after the mid-fifth century, but the city was surely overrun by conquerors on their way south to the capital. A second sack of Rome itself took place when Genseric the Vandal arrived in 455 and the titular emperors fled to swamp-circled Ravenna on the Adriatic coast with what was left of their authority. There Gothic and Barbarians became Christians and built churches, fixing their gaze on the life of another world that was displayed in their mosaic-covered walls.

While they lived in a spiritual preoccupation, eschewing conquest and the establishment of a larger order, they kept Bologna as a dependency in the immediate west where the town was in the line of battle with the Langobards, who later came down to take over the northern part of the Po valley.

God knows what happened in the sixth, seventh, and eighth centuries. More than a dozen generations of men and women were born, grew up, fell in love, toiled, had children, and died without leaving a single mark on any page we can find today. Almost none could read or write. Many faced a wretched end in war or a lingering death from infection after a sword wound from an invader, or even more slowly from famine. Some lives began in the violence of rape. We know next to nothing of these people except that most found what comfort there was in some form of Christianity. They took strength from the saints whose intercession they sought, especially from the endearing archetype, Mary, the Mother of God. If these ages were truly dark and obscure, devotion to her seems to have provided what light there was. But I know too that there were spring days and hours of real sunshine in northern Italy then as now. Surely there must have been some love and laughter, for there were children born to the dwellers in Emilia-Romagna whose descendants today populate Bologna and its surrounding countryside. In the town and its attendant churches, priests, however badly schooled, were celebrating Mass in some form or other in the eighth century when Charlemagne stayed there on his way south to get himself crowned by the pope in AD 800.

Walls around the little city were required many years earlier, perhaps in the fifth century, as soon as the central command of the Roman legions disappeared in Italy. But by the Middle Ages (AD 500 to 800), the general slash-and-grab style of political and commercial life even required defensive structures inside the town. Towers were built as part of the houses of the well-to-do; before long they were tall enough to be well beyond the range of scaling ladders. There are about forty stubs of an original several hundred towers in Bologna, and several are of enormous proportion.

By the eleventh century a pair of hostile families, the Asinelli and the Garisenda, had produced a huge pair directly in the path of the old Roman road which actually passed between them. One family was Guelph (favoring the pope's political interest) and the other Ghibelline (betting on the Holy Roman Emperor). The Asinelli tower is 318 feet in height. We don't know the original altitude of its rival because early on it began to settle on one side and developed an alarming tilt. To avoid the inevitable crash, the Garisenda was

DUE TORRE Bologna   C. 1120

dismantled from the top down until the reduced mass stopped settling. The lower tower remains a paltry 155 feet high, set at a rakish angle. The taller of the pair tilts a bit too, but not so you would complain much about it.

Today the *Due Torre* are the symbols of Bologna, sprouting from the heart of the city, leaning more or less away from each other like a pair of slightly hostile barroom customers contemplating a fight. You surely know you are in the capital of Emilia-Romagna when you see them above you.

During the prosperous growth of the cities of northern Italy in the Renaissance, most, with or without an asparagus patch of residential towers on the inside, became large walled enclosures with elaborate and broad battlements surrounding them. Towns were built to withstand a yearlong siege, or worse. At about the same time that modern explosive artillery shells rendered the walls less useful for defense, the other results of the Industrial Revolution began to provide support for a larger population. There came a need for new factory buildings, multiple dwellings, and the network of railroads that now connect what had been warring cities of earlier centuries. This sequence produced a pattern that still exists in many of the northern cities: a compact, walled old city (*il centro storico*) surrounded by a ring of industry which is, in turn, contained within a circle of twentieth-century suburbs. The building of the railroads in the nineteenth century allowed the location of railroad stations at the perimeter of the old city, usually a fifteen-minute bus ride from the duomo in the cathedral square at the center of it all. Demolition of the fortifications in some towns (such as Modena) created a park-like ring of boulevards that follow the original route of the walls. In nineteenth-century Vienna, on the other side of the Alps, the *Ringstrasse* encircles the whole medieval city and provided (besides a double tram line) such an elegant location for so many civic buildings that it gave rise to a whole style of public architecture named for that boulevard.

We got instructions for finding our hotel on the Via Montegrappa from the helpful folks at the tourist office in the railroad station and set forth on a bus. Every town in Italy has streets named for Mazzini, Garibaldi, and Cavour, as well as piazzas remembering Victor Emmanuel or memorable dates like the 8th of August or the 20th of September. But here we traversed the Via Guglielmo Marconi (a local boy who went on to invent the radio) and then turned into the Via Ugo Bassi (named for a heroic left-wing priest who was executed in 1849), which turned out to be the local name for a few blocks of the ancient Via Emilia. This is the original Roman road along which the Renaissance cities of the Po valley are strung like pearls on the bosom of the fertile plain, Rimini, Forlì, Bologna, Modena, Reggio, Parma, Piacenza, and, eventually, Milano.

In Bologna it seems agreed upon that everyone should go about the city looking one's best. Shoes gleam, jackets are chic, and hosiery is sheer and spectacularly in evidence at nearly full length. Bologna is a town in which it is good for an adult male tourist to wear a reasonably expensive necktie. Without one you might be taken for a German tourist or an American one. I sometimes thought we received slightly more tolerant service and more of a sense of a familiar relationship with Italians by taking on the protective coloration of respectable, upper-middle-class English. I suspect that this congeniality dates back to some good experiences with Albion in the seventeenth and eighteenth centuries, or a lingering fascination with Lord Byron's extended stay in the nineteenth. This was in marked contrast to the rough handling Italy received from the French and Austrians in the same period of time. Of course, the Anglo-Saxon cover can be blown in an instant when ordering a gin martini with lots of ice (*molto ghiaccio*) at 5:30 or 6:00 in the afternoon.

We dismounted across from the Piazza Roosevelt and looked down the length of the straight section of the Roman road to the two great towers leaning each way, where V. Ugo Bassi becomes V. Rizzoli. Both sides of the street have colonnades of either Romanesque or Gothic arches built right out to the street. Shop windows are along the interior wall of the covered space, brightly lit and full of the best of contemporary Italian manufacture. One seldom needs an umbrella in Bologna; there are many miles of colonnades in the old city.

Our hotel, a dignified and often-remodeled pile—in an unbeatable location—had an English name: The Palace (pronounced in the Italian fashion with three syllables: *Pa / la / cé*), and featured a club-like lobby bar and two elevators. The Palace is on the street named for Ugo Bassi, the martyred priest who preached Italian independence from Austria while following Garibaldi. He was shot and is rightly considered a martyr in the cause of the Risorgimento. This hotel was not the best bargain we found to be acceptable in our first tour, but we judged (rightly, in retrospect) that we should find comfortable landing places in the beginning and then seek economy as we got more used to the country. As far as we could tell, a government rating of even one star seems to guarantee a clean room, but a limited supply of towels and virtually nothing else. Two stars turned out to signal a perfectly good accommodation wherever we went, and the advantages of a third star amounted only to the presence of the color television set, slightly more space for a baggage rack, a mini-fridge filled with carefully counted tiny bottles of international name-brand booze, and, downstairs, a somewhat snappier lounge off the lobby. The Palace gets three stars, and in 2008 cost about 170 U.S. dollars per night.

We never bothered to learn of the unknown delights of four- or five-star hotels since, except for a bit of Italian TV, all the two extra stars promised was an alarming increase in the price of a night's accommodation. I don't think their *cornetti con marmellatta and caffelatte* could have been any better than those we experienced.[1]

Late in the day we found a nice *pasticceria* just off the Via Emilia. It had an upper room with low arched windows looking out on a busy crossing. I ordered a gin and tonic and a martini made to my own formula, *mezzo mezzo con vermouth e gin inglese.* I like Martini & Rossi dry vermouth if the bottle is recently opened, which it usually is in Italy. I think we left the waiter guessing where we came from: Quebec? Copenhagen?

After our *aperitivo*, by 7:30 (the earliest possible hour to find a *ristorante* or *trattoria* open) we came down to street level and went in search of dinner. Among the streets behind the Palace Hotel we found an unprepossessing trattoria that was already filling with guests. Our table was across from a group of four Bolognese who had a sort of university air about them. All were at least middle-aged, and they seemed to focus on an older man of professorial mien with pure white hair and a florid complexion. He also had huge white eyebrows that overhung his spectacles to the extent that when he looked down at his plate, his eyes disappeared entirely behind their snow-white bushyness. When he raised his head after a spoonful of his tortellini, the eyes flashed out and the crinkling crows' feet emphasized his smile.

The other man at the table wore an impeccable houndstooth jacket and an expensive necktie. The two women were comfortably

---

[1] Cities the size of Bologna, Milan, and Venice are more expensive than smaller cities like Cremona, Modena, or Verona. In general, rates were less than in comparable quarters found while touring the U.S. And when it comes to waterfront towns, I'll take Venice over Chicago any day. Bologna has frequent trade fairs that can make hotel reservations hard to come by.

elegant. Not being able to understand their conversation was a considerable frustration, and we resolved to get on with the business of learning to handle more rapidly spoken Italian.

We followed their lead and had marvelous *tortellini in brodo* followed by grilled sole and fresh spinach perfumed with a touch of garlic and olive oil. Fish is wonderful all over Italy; no one is far from the sea.

Bologna is known as *Il Grasso* or *Il Dotto* depending upon whether one is more impressed with the town's learning or its food. There are lots of bookstores, especially around the corner from the towers and down along the Via Zamboni where the university lecture halls are located. We spent a happy afternoon browsing in several and found a treasure trove of parallel translation editions of a number of standard English classics. Reading Coleridge's "The Rhyme of the Ancient Mariner" or T. S. Eliot's "The Waste Land" in Italian with the English original on the facing page is a great way to expand the vocabulary with useful words and memorable phrases.

We bought a half-dozen books and had them shipped home by surface mail, a pleasant reminder of our visit which arrived a month after we got home.

The geometric, legal, civic, artistic, and religious center of Bologna is the Piazza Maggiore, which is bounded by the Basilica of St. Petronius, the Palazzo Comunale, the Palazzo del Podesta, and an essential row of green grocers, butcher shops, and fish markets that have been located on the north side of the square since medieval times. In the sixteenth century a very capable architect, Vignola, was hired to dignify the area by concealing the shops without cutting off access to them. He did a splendid job of it with his Palazzo Banchi, a long and narrow four-story facade composed of fifteen arches, several of which lead to open passageways into the old market warren behind.

The buildings around the piazza are a wonderful example of architectural styles from the twelfth through the later sixteenth centuries. They go together without the slightest hint of disharmony. Imagine a city center today ringed with buildings by Christopher Wren, Louis Sullivan, Stanford White, and I. M. Pei, all somewhat closer to each other in time, and expecting the result to uplift the spirit and give you the sense that you really are someplace. I suppose it comes from some deep-seated sense of politeness with which architects regarded their forefathers a few centuries ago.[3]

The Basilica of St. Petronius is the oldest, biggest, and most interesting of the buildings facing the square. Interestingly, it was never designed to be a cathedral and never became one in spite of being the largest church and the biggest building in town. It is about the twelfth part of a mile-long inside (132 meters) and nearly 200 feet wide. Inside the nave the arches supporting the roof are joined almost 150 feet over your head. The usual design of a Gothic cathedral was cruciform, but St. Petronius was built without transepts and thus turned out to be more or less a basilica in shape. We heard that the addition of transepts would have made the church rival the early St. Peter's in size; and the then-reigning pope took steps to prevent this by diverting money that might have gone into the building to other worthy causes.

Whether this story is true or not, the Bolognese neither really finished their principal church building, nor gave up the notion that they were only part of the way through the project until well after World War II. Then, in a fit of humility and perhaps of obedience to papal desire, they declared the work complete and got the

---

[2] Philip Johnson's propped-up storefront facade (of limestone!) across from the Metropolitan Museum in New York shows how the contemporary self-publicizing architect will respond if asked to do something in harmony with surrounding buildings of an earlier style. We don't have to wonder what Vignola would have done in like circumstances. It's right there on the opposite side of the Piazza Maggiore.

church consecrated in 1954, well over half a millennium after they had laid the cornerstone.

The finished marble skin of the front of the building only covers the lowest third of the brickwork, leaving the stark understructure standing gaunt and bare above.

But as much of the facade as was finished is truly splendid! Started in the late fourteenth century, its instructive decoration was begun early in the *quattrocento*[3] by Jacopo della Quercia, one of the earliest of the great Renaissance masters of sculpture. Jacopo made both freestanding figures and deeply modeled bas-reliefs in framed panels around the center doorway. The creamy white marble figures suggest the full, round productions of the Greeks

---

[3] Italians have a unique method of designating centuries. While formally designating the fifteenth century as *il quindicesimo secolo*, they speak more familiarly of the period as the *quattrocento*, ignoring the first thousand years of the Christian era. I suppose that when one has such an abundance of centuries to deal with as do the scholars and inhabitants of the peninsula, it is only to be expected that they should call their familiars by nicknames.

two millennia before his time. Like his Gothic predecessors, he tells the story of the creation and fall of man, but his figures are from another world. To understand the real impact his work had on this period, you should first see the naked twelfth-century Adam and Eve on the facade of the duomo of Modena. They clutch their fig leaves in attitudes of dejection, shame, and terror. Jacopo's primal parents are different, careless of their beauty and their nakedness before their sin.

Even while they are being expelled from Eden, and Eve is ineffectually shielding her body with her hands, Adam almost seems to put up a fight and contend with the angel. Later still, barely clothed, he digs his garden with a right good will. His wife holds a distaff well loaded with spun wool and regards her husband with an admiring expectation of his success in bringing home the bacon. The two children grasp at their mother's knees like any pair of contemporary kids begging for access to the candy rack in the supermarket checkout line.[4]

None of the Renaissance artists were a bit embarrassed about the details of nudity, either male or female. From Neptune in his fountain to the Bambino in the arms of his mother, or as an adult Christ half-submerged in the limpid waters of baptism, male nakedness seems appropriate in their art. Michelangelo painted a naked Christ judging the living and the dead in the Sistine Chapel, although his loins were subsequently shrouded in a swirl of protective drapery at the command of a later pope. And, of course, there are the *putti,* thousands of them, always male and always quite

---

[4] No reproductions of the great works of art really look like the originals. My sketches aren't intended to do so anymore than a four-color print can resemble a Mantegna painting. They are included to help indulgent readers identify what I am writing about.

mother-naked, coursing about the ceilings and picture frames of the later centuries of Italian painting. Breasts are another matter; they seem relegated to the prediluvian or at least pre-Christian world, except in the case of St. Agnes who carries hers, rather gruesomely, on a plate.

Naming the great church for Petronius seemed odd to us at first. We had never heard of him before coming to Bologna and couldn't see why he rated such prominence. He is in the books as having been bishop from 431 to 450, just about the end of the civilized Roman period and the start of the dark age in Italy. His biography was composed about 700 years later and lacks the smack of firsthand observation. It is maintained that he re-founded the town after the Emperor Theodosius destroyed it. He is also credited with founding the university around the same time, but everybody doubts this. The beginnings of learned Bologna may be lost in the mists of time, but they are not that old. Still, by the mid-thirteenth century the city was having a party in honor of Petronius on October fourth each year, and he has been considered the principal saint of Bologna since then. By 1388 the people of the free town decreed a great church in his honor—not a cathedral, but a civic and religious center. Its location on the surface of the globe is reliably defined by a white marble stripe in the pink stone floor of the basilica that traces the true north/south line of the meridian.[5]

---

[5] The line was laid out by Giovanni Domenico Cassini in the middle of the seventeenth century. Cassini was one of the great observers in the early days of the telescope. He found a hatful of satellites around Saturn as well as the largest division in its ring system. He taught astronomy at the University, but when he became famous he was tempted away to the Paris observatory by the emoluments offered by Louis XIV. Later he found the polar caps of Mars, and, by timing their rotation and comparing data from America, made a pretty good estimate of the distance between the earth and the sun. Never having been a fan of the *L'état c'est moi* school of monarchy, I rather wish he had stayed on as a faculty member at Bologna.

There is lots to see in the enormous basilica, especially the pair of frescoed crucifixes by Giovanni da Modena. He also supplied a wonderful cycle on the Three Kings. Some of the reliquaries containing bits and pieces of the holy (including the head of Petronius) are curiously contrived. The high Gothic polychromed wood carving is wholly unlike della Quercia's great Renaissance doorway. But for all its distance from his or our time and place, it speaks more clearly to me than the late baroque and rococo stuff that came along a few hundred years later. The tomb of Napoleon's sister looks like something from another planet as, I guess, he and his family really were.

The church has two enormous organs which face each other across the choir. They were built about 125 years apart in the fifteenth and sixteenth centuries. A lot of music has been composed for the pair. We missed hearing them going with all stops out. I'd like to go back someday to hear what they can do on a feast day.

During one of our trips in the mid-1990s, we noticed the stolid, depressed gypsy women seated at the doorways with their cardboard signs proclaiming that they were Yugoslavian refugees. I am always hesitant about beggars. Most seem too professional for my pity. On the other hand I am a lot better off than they, and begging for the meager purchasing power of those fractional Italian coins is a very difficult way to earn a living. Even if they are good at it, they aren't getting rich.

High on the wall of the Municipal Palace, stage left of the basilica, there is a glowing terracotta Madonna holding up her perfect Child for all to acknowledge. It was done by Niccolo dell'Arca in 1478, the date displayed in large Roman numerals across the corbeled pedestal she rests on. The brilliance implied by the modeled rays on the background seem to come from the child Himself. His mother, much the larger figure, seems to be a background making him visible to us but in no way calling attention to herself. She is as lovely and as modern as any of the Bolognese girls coming through the square on their way to class. Niccolo's idea of the perfection of this "sole boast of our fallen race" speaks through time without any diminution at all. He got it right: she's as good as they come. Art, as usual, is far more persuasive than theology.

Around the corner of the agreeable bulk of the Palazzo del Podestà is a little *piazzetta*, a sort of panhandle to the Piazza Maggiore. From it you can look at that part of the Podesta called the Palace of King Enzo. Enzo wasn't king of Bologna; far from it. He was the beloved illegitimate son of the H.R. Emperor Frederick II.[6] He was also King of Sardinia. His horse was killed under him at the Battle of Fossalto in 1249 when the Modenese were vanquished by the Bolognese, and he was captured along with a lot of valuable loot, some German soldiers, and three thousand other prisoners. His father promised "enough silver to circle the walls of Bologna" to get him back unharmed, but the Bolognese kept him for the rest of his life. The royal hostage gave them greater security than any city wall could provide. He was locked up in state in the Podesta Palace in a couple of rooms that looked out on the *piazzetta*, then empty save for the pigeons that perpetually feed there. Only twenty-two at the time, he understandably found the confinement trying even though he was treated and served as a king. Once, after who knows how long in the royal slammer, he saw a beautiful girl feeding the pigeons in the square below his barred window. An introduction

---

[6] Frederick was considered the wonder of the world in the thirteenth century. He has gone down in the books as *Stupor Mundi*, an appellation of intriguing innuendo, but he was indeed a fascinating man; see my account of him in *About Sicily*.

was arranged by one of the Asinelli. (You remember the family that built the taller tower?) Her name was Lucia. When introduced to the damsel, the young king, taking what must have been considered a rather direct approach even in those days, said *Anima mia, ben ti voglio!* ('Pon my soul, how I desire you!) Thus, when she later bore a son, the bambino, being illegitimate, was given the surname Bentivoglio. From him sprang the line of dukes that ruled Bologna for the greater part of the Middle Ages and the early Renaissance. After all, they were descended from a king, even if he was one who spent most of his life in captivity. Actually, I think the Bolognese were quite nice to allow him the company of a young woman of such legendary attractiveness. I hope they were pleased with the resulting rulers they acquired therefrom in future years.

A few hundred years after the royal prisoner's romantic assignations, the Bentivoglios being fully in charge, and the Renaissance passion for classical mythology having temporarily supplanted the outdoor display of saints, angels, and the Madonna, a huge statue of Neptune was commissioned to ornament the little square. It was done by a French sculptor, Jean Boulogne, who, unlike Cassini, gave an Italian form to his name: Giambologna.

The father of the oceans stands relaxed, enjoying his broad-shouldered nakedness in sunshine, rain, or snow. There is a mature grace to his hefty body, powerful but not muscle-bound; his weight is on his left leg, his right foot scratches the back of a gamboling pet dolphin. He surmounts a pedestal of rosy Verona marble, holds his trident lightly, and gestures mysteriously with his left hand. The Bolognese call him *il Gigante*.

Beneath Neptune are a group of bronze *putti*, usually with pigeons ornamenting their curly heads. Below them a quartet of immense metal mermaids (or perhaps harpies) squat facing the four corners of a huge marble basin. Unlike more conventional mermaids, these have divided thighs covered with bronze scales terminating in paired fish tails. They clutch and seem to squeeze their breasts from which sprays of water provide an allegory for the mythical rivers of antiquity. The whole is decorated with the armorial bearings of Pope Pius IV, considered to be an enlightened ruler of the city, and obviously a patron of catholic taste.

We visited a score of churches in Bologna. Here, as in all of Italy, they are the repositories of the great art and are museums

"IL GIGANTE" - BOLOGNA
1563

without entrance fees. They also keep museum hours: most of them close for two to three hours after lunch, giving us another good reason to plan our itineraries in order to get back to the hotel for our own nap (*pisolino*), when most of the rest of the town is shut down anyway.

Among the best of the Bolognese churches is the architectural melange known as the Basilica of Santo Stefano. The earliest of this collection of seven separate small churches is attributed to Ambrose of Milan, who had it built in 392 to house the relics of saints Vitale and Agricola, which he discovered in the Jewish cemetery. I wonder what inspired him to dig there? In the middle of the next century, St. Petronius added a small church copying the design of the Holy Sepulcher in Jerusalem. The Langobards (Christians by then) continued to enlarge the cluster of buildings after they fought their way into the town in 727. Although much restored and changed over the millennia, these are impressively ancient places of worship. Charlemagne stopped here to hear Mass on his way to Rome. He graciously repaid the local monks by gathering up a number of their relics and sending them home to France.[7]

It is hard for us today to imagine the importance of relics of the saints to the Christians of earlier ages. There is a legitimate economic theory that much of the trade between countries before and during the Dark Ages and the Crusades took place

---

[7] From Charlemagne through Napoleon, French rulers of many different centuries have practiced this method of enriching their palaces, churches, and museums. The Louvre is full of stolen Italian treasures. This record of larceny is quite unlike the record of the English and American collectors who, starting with Charles I and carrying on to Benjamin Altman, bought the stuff when the Italians felt they had lots of art anyway and needed the money more. The French record of cultural conservation is further blotched by their gunners, who had a habit of using large works of art—such as the Sphinx in the nineteenth century, and Leonardo da Vinci's clay model for an equestrian statue of a former Duke of Milan in the sixteenth—as objects for target practice.

coincidentally along with the buying and selling of bones, teeth, hair, and other body parts of holy people of prior ages. I have heard a story of a whole city being sacked in order to facilitate the recovery of the tooth of St. Matthew from a perfidious Sicilian who had provided a bogus relic as part of the town's ransom. His fraud was discovered when the false relic didn't work to restore the warrior's sick child to health.

We approached the Basilica of St. Dominic with our noses in the map. Inside this thirteenth-century building we found architecture of the eighteenth century and the extraordinary reliquary of the founder of the Order of Preachers. Dominic Guzman was a Spaniard and a university graduate. Both in his life and in the work of the order he founded, he was the counterbalance to St. Francis who provided the emotional inspiration of the later Middle Ages. Dominic preached to the people, using all the resources of his intellect to persuade and convert. Francis, God's troubador, rushed to embrace them.

Dominic's container is termed an ark, and it is indeed an extraordinary vessel. Most of his remains are buried about halfway up the cream, buff, and pearly white, twenty-foot stack of medieval, Renaissance, and baroque marble. The front of the sarcophagus itself was done by Nicola Pisano around 1265. Down below is an altar that has a large eighteenth-century front panel with scenes from the saint's life done in the early 1530s. On the altar level are a pair of angels bearing candlesticks, one by Niccolo of Antonio and the other by Michelangelo, who was about fifteen years old when he got the commission in the 1490s. Up above there is more *quattrocento* work, including Michelangelo's St. Proculus, which looks quite a bit like his later David, with clothes on. The top of the ark is decorated with cascades of fruit and *putti* that date from the late baroque. Although at first glance the ark is reminiscent of a wedding cake, the individual sculptures and reliefs are so wonderful that they overcome the whipped-cream look of the whole.

We were guided through the side chapels and other rooms off the apse of the huge building by an elderly, very dignified guide, a sort of verger, I guess, who lectured us in clear and simple Italian about what we were seeing. He took us into the retrochoir behind the main altar and showed us the amazing intarsia panels behind the choir stalls. This extensive series of wooden inlays displays a fresh and facile draftsmanship that would be hard to match with pen or pencil, but was actually done in thousands of tiny pieces of wood, cut, shaped, and glued to provide a complete spectrum of shades, colors, and forms. Brother Daminiano of Bergamo, who did them, was a discovery for us. We had never heard of this sixteenth-century master who spent more than twenty years decorating these choir stalls.

Our courtly guide then unlocked the sacristy museum and showed us still other treasures, including representations of St. Dominic as fat and St. Thomas Aquinas as lean—quite the opposite of their actual figures, I believe.

I was unable to figure out the precise role of our elderly guide. As we were leaving the locked end of the building I pressed a couple thousand lira notes into his hand. He accepted them without protest, but I then saw him deposit them in an alms box as he walked away, making me feel like the classic crude, rich American tourist who missed the point: He was working for love. His courtesy and his dignity bespoke religious conviction as well as human kindness. Some men become pious in their later years; some become scholarly. A few become both, as did this grand old man who led us through the treasures of the basilica.

Although it is not appointed with painting and sculpture as the churches are, it seems to me that the real spiritual center of Bologna is the Archiginnasio. Although it dates only from the sixteenth century, this is the earliest surviving building that houses the university. No one really knows when the Alma Mater Studiorum began, and for centuries it really had no permanent buildings of its own. Sometime, probably well before the year 1000, perhaps as early as 890, students gathered in Bologna and hired scholars to lecture and teach them the remembered principles of Roman law. The university was both old and famous before the first half of the twelfth century when young Thomas à Becket came to study. So did Dante, Petrarch, and (coming from Poland) Copernicus. The entire conduct of the school was for centuries in the hands of the students, who allowed the faculty only the authority to grant degrees, an arrangement that would have horrified American college administrators if it had even been suggested by the "radical" students of the 1960s. There are reputed to be something like 65,000 students currently enrolled in all the faculties, making the old Alma Mater Studiorum by far the biggest enterprise in Bologna.

The halls and loggias of the Archiginnasio are decorated with thousands of the coats of arms of young men who studied there over the years.[8] This seems a much more civilized way of leaving a memento of one's passing than carving a set of initials in the wood-work of Old South Main, but both stem from the same impulse to

---

[8] There were women, too, although I don't know if any left coats of arms on the soffits of the hallways. Women were also professors of the law. Shakespeare's Portia would have presented no surprise when she pretended to be a learned, if youthful, *dottoressa* of the law.

eternalize the "shortest, gladdest years of life." The most exciting room of all turns out to be a reconstruction: the Teatro Anatomica, which took a direct hit from an Allied bomb in World War II. The building was destroyed, but, amazingly enough, among the splintered remains were found a number of the wooden sculptures that adorned it, including the damaged but salvageable studies of "skinned" men, their full musculature observable to the students. All the pieces were gathered up, and from existing drawings and plans, the famous old medical school room was put back in its original form, with bare pine and cedar walls detailed into elegantly classical panels and pilasters. Somehow there seems to be no touch of Williamsburg or Disney in any reconstruction in Italy. It is, after all, the very spot where the modern study of anatomy really began, where the theoretical scholasticism of medieval medicine began to give way to scientific investigation.

When the great minds of the Renaissance started to search inward for the mysteries of the body and to look out beyond the bounds of our planet, they had to get through the boundaries set up by an unsettled and somewhat nervous medieval church, many of whose leaders saw the new learning as a powerful deterrent to obedience at the least and a deterrent to faith itself at the worst. While Rome forbade dissection of cadavers—presumably as a matter of theological certainty that all the parts would be needed for use again after the last trumpet had sounded—the Bolognese took a different course. The bodies of executed criminals were given to the university medical faculty to be dissected on a marble slab in the middle of the room while as many as several hundred medical students watched from the ranks of raised benches.

From positions on the faculties of the old universities of Pisa, Padua, Bologna, and others, astronomers like Galileo looked out upon a newly discovered universe and anatomists peered deep within the human body. Both were undeterred by the strictures of the timid orthodoxy of their time. And learning such as theirs, once out of the box, cannot be confined again.

X

CRIME IN ITALY
Probably No Worse than What You Are Used To

We did not experience a theft, mugging, holdup, swindle, or con job in any of our trips to northern Italy. Our first visit to Rome, however, featured an encounter with a group of gypsy pickpocketing girls and an unknown perpetrator (probably a very young one) who broke into our rental car to steal a box of *cioccolatini*. Many Italians told us the South is where most of the crime occurs in the country. Surely Sicily is the home court of the *Cosa Nostra*, the self-given name of the Mafia, but the Mafia isn't organizing to eliminate the tourist trade just now; they have too many other things on their plate to contend with.

An encounter with an outlaw is something that makes Americans (especially senior Americans) uncertain about traveling in a foreign country without guide or escort. We have concluded that in northern Italy at least, there is less street crime than we are used to in America. In Rome and the South it may be different, which is one reason we put off visiting there until we were better at speaking the language and reading the local climate. We felt very safe in Tuscany, Emilia, Lombardy, Venice, and Umbria, and eventually, in Puglia and Sicily as well.

Concerning a violent attack on your person, the possibility of encountering a killer, or at least one who might kill you, is extremely remote and nearly nonexistent if you take the minimal precautions you would follow in New York or Boston.

We noted that there seem to be very few "drive-by" shootings. Italians have a much, much harder time laying their hands on guns of any sort than do Americans. They are simply not for sale in the stores. Hunting shotguns, mostly single-chambered, are around in the country, but the twenty-year-old unemployed city kid almost never has one. Handguns are so expensive and strictly controlled that only the successful and gainfully employed would be likely to have one. This doesn't mean that Italians don't shoot, strangle, or stab each other; it just means that they don't often do these things with strangers.

In his exuberant book *The Italians*, Luigi Barzini points out that Italians have a considerable fear of sudden death themselves, but the reasons for this anxiety are quite predictable:

> *The vigorous passions of a turbulent and restless people are always ready to flare up unexpectedly like hot coals under the ashes. Italy is a blood-stained country. Almost every day of the year jealous husbands kill their adulterous wives and their lovers; about as many wives kill their adulterous husbands and their mistresses; fathers or older brothers kill the seducers of defenseless and guileless virgins, virgins kill the men trying to rape them; desperate young lovers commit suicide together in pairs, or separately one at a time. This steady massacre, inspired by love, which has been going on for centuries, has surely cost more lives than the many pestilences and catastrophes which have ravaged the country, and the wars fought on Italian soil.*

Tourism is thus far less dangerous in Italy than a love relationship or a family tie. Newspapers report a few spectacular crimes wherein the world of vice pays its debts with a strangling scarf or stiletto. Prostitutes and their pimps often do each other in, and an occasional irate taxpayer takes on a tax collector. There are more than a few earthquakes, but these can happen in California and, as far as the rest of America is concerned, tornadoes and hurricanes hardly ever happen.

So, barring the collapse of the surface of the planet in the area you are visiting, there is a simple rule that will keep you in the statistically safest fraction of the population: avoid romantic entanglement with anyone of either sex or of any age, except your own dear spouse, and your personal safety will increase by a large factor. If you travel with your significant other, you will almost surely be safer than if you go it alone.

As it turns out, usually the only criminals the tourist has to be on the lookout for are (1) the pairs of athletic young bag snatchers on Vespas or other *motorini*, and (2) children between the ages of nine and twelve.

The first type cruises the crowded and narrow streets of the busier parts of Rome and Naples with the grabber on the back of the *motorino*, while the pilot threads his way through the pedestrians looking for a likely tourist's handbag carried over the outboard shoulder. When the rider grabs one, the pilot roars off and is soon around the corner and out of sight. The best defense is to keep the handbag strap over both head and shoulder on the building side of the sidewalk. As a pair, it makes sense for a woman with such a bag not to walk on the curb side.

The second type of street theft is more common and easier to deal with if you are prepared. The culprits are frequently the gypsy children, often preadolescent girls, who approach from the front holding up a newspaper or a picture as if to show you something of interest. While the paper is in front of your line of sight, the other girls circle to the rear and two or three together will simultaneously pick your pockets. It happens very quickly. The first time I was approached by these children I was surprised, but instinctively shot my left hand into my inner breast pocket to secure my wallet. In the pocket I found the hand of a child which I managed to grasp by the fingers and extract. Twisting a little girl's fingers with one hand while gripping my wallet with the other seemed such an unlikely thing for a sixty-five-year-old grandfather to be doing that I let her go with a great shout while my wife whacked at her with a short, furled umbrella. After it was all over, the street vendors of postcards (we were close to the Colosseum) gave encouraging shouts of outrage, but we noted that they had given no sign of warning when they saw the little gypsy band approach us. We learned that if a child approaches with a picture, magazine, or newspaper in hand, glare, growl, be ready to spit, and shove the tyke away before he or she gets within pocket reach. A savage response to the most innocently childish face is a wise precaution.

We also learned to leave nothing in the rental car. Locking an empty car up tight invites breaking into it, and, since it is a rental, theft of the whole car is not an insuperable problem. I once parked on the Aventine Hill in Rome while painting a watercolor sketch of the Tiber below. Forty minutes later, I came back to find the right rear window of the Panda broken, and the canvas cover of the luggage trunk cut open. The only thing missing was a box of Perrugino Bacci—chocolate kisses wrapped in silver paper that we were planning to bring home to our own children. The aforementioned preadolescent *banditi* had struck!

Precautions against pickpockets are easy to make. My wife wore a necklace wallet with a stainless steel chain underneath her turtleneck traveling blouse. The little leather portfolio was just large enough for her passport, a couple of credit cards, and some folding money. Upscale leather goods shops in the U.S. carry them.

Money belts also work, but my own method is slightly more elaborate and more comfortable. I had a tailor make four-by-eight inch vertical pockets that could be secured to the inside of my trouser waistband with three buttons. My passport case with credit cards, large denomination bills, and airline tickets go down inside the belt, inside the trousers, into the deep pocket where they can be gotten at by me alone, with some difficulty at that. I carry some ready cash in a smaller billfold in my inside jacket pocket. So far, after seventeen visits, we have never been robbed of anything while in Italy, except for that one pretty box of chocolates.

Italy has at least four different police forces, and I suspect there are others with still more gorgeous uniforms that I am not familiar with. The local traffic cops are *vigili urbani*, a large number of whom speak pretty good English. A special force for financial crime and counterfeiting whose title escapes me are in evidence at the portals of large banks and are well armed. The *polizia urbana* is the local anticriminal force. The *carabinieri*, a division of the army that carries submachine guns as well as 9mm pistols, are the elite of law enforcement. They are almost always seen in pairs, and look threatening but always seem to turn a smiling face toward us. Most speak pretty good English. Venice and other port towns also have a considerable presence of the Coast Guard, or *Guardia Costiera*, but we decided we would not ever get to meet them unless we came in our own boat.

We learned the words to shout: *Ladro! Ladro! Aiutarmi! Polizia!* just in case. But we also learned not to worry about it any more than we would at home in Connecticut or North Carolina.

XI

MODENA
Home of Ferrari, Maserati, and Pavarotti

Many of the larger churches of Emilia-Romagna have lion porches, but those of Modena were the first and are still the most charming. Lovers sit beside them on the sunny south side of the cathedral in autumn, children ride them like pet St. Bernards, tourists photograph them, passing townspeople caress their heads on their way in or out of church. They are present at both the main and the two south-side doorways, as well as inside where they hold up a splendid rood screen that dates from the late 1190s.

The campanile, which is freestanding off the north corner of the building, is a mighty spire called *la Ghirlandina*, the little garland or wreath, an affectionate diminutive that refers to a bronze wreath on the weathervane which is almost three hundred feet above your head as you stand in the square. The tower is visible for miles around and very much the symbol of the town. It was completed in 1310, and is another of those heroic feats of medieval engineering and architecture that make me wonder if we have really learned much of anything new since the fourteenth century. Inside we noted that the ceiling arches actually function as trusses rather than the barrel vaults and groins more common in the period.

WEST PORCH - MODENA

As a whole, Modena's *duomo* is the best example of Lombard Romanesque architecture we encountered. Lanfranco, who designed it, was an innovator, and his patroness, Contessa Matilda of Canossa, gave him plenty of room to experiment. The twelfth-century sculptor Wiligelmo and his students decorated the exterior in the chaste Lombard style of their time. The carvings appear to grow on the stone supporting members, making this as good an example of integrated design, detailing, and decoration as you will ever see. I'd say that Modena's duomo is right up there with the nearly contemporary Durham Cathedral in Yorkshire as a candidate for "best building."

We came to Modena[1] feeling in need of slightly better quarters than we'd had the past several nights. We reserved at a three-star hotel

---

[1] The name of the town is one of the many exceptions to the generalization that Italian names are accented penultimately. The stress is on the first syllable.

with a disproportionately modest tariff, the Libertà, on the Via Blasius in the block immediately north of the duomo. It turned out also to have its own garage. Although we didn't need it, we made note of its presence, since very few of the hotels in the old town centers have secure parking for cars. The Libertà also had very modern beds, color TV, contemporary furnishings in the lobby, bar, and breakfast room. Even the plumbing was right up-to-date. The train trip was short, and, since we arrived in the middle of the day, we set out to scope out the cathedral early in the afternoon.

Later, when we checked the news, we saw a sorrowful anchor reporting what the newspapers had been printing for several days: Federico Fellini was gravely ill and seemed to be sinking.

The Harvard guidebook recommended Trattoria da Omer just across the parklet near the Libertà. We got a reservation through the good offices of the desk clerk, but we didn't realize how early one must book at the Omer. It is an inexpensive and very popular place to enjoy Emilian food. Signora Omer was manning the *cassa* when we arrived, busy tying little knots in the handmade tortellini. She also welcomed her guests, brought the menus, served the wine, and waited on tables. Her husband, who did all the cooking, was tangentially visible in his immaculate whites and gleaming kitchen. I think they had a pot walloper out in back to do the dishes, but other than that, it was strictly a family affair. We were served a plate of just three large, plump ravioli containing a collection of rare cheeses, under a pale pink Emilian sauce with a colorful garnish of thinly sculptured red and green bell pepper. It was just about as delicious as anything I have ever eaten. For a *secondo* we had some mysterious and ambrosial pork slices and spinach that had been brought to worthy attention by quite a lot of garlic and a trace of

the famous Modenese balsamic vinegar. After that first experience
we tried to go back the following night, but we couldn't get in. If
you go there, reserve early for the following night just to be sure.

We noted in an older edition of the Harvard guidebook that a
"heart-wrenching depiction of Adam and Eve being evicted from the
Garden of Eden" was to the left of the main door of the cathedral.
We stopped to study it, having become *affezionati* of such scenes from
our other experiences in Verona, Orvieto, and Bologna. Modena's
expulsion is a first-class twelfth-century depiction in stone, but to my
mind is surpassed by the horror of Cain bashing Abel over the head
with an enormous truncheon in the neighboring panel. This is the
same work that was presented to the youthful vision of Jacopo della
Quercia as he wrestled with his vision of Greeks and Romans, fusing
them in the amazing creation panels at San Petronius. The major
museums of Modena are happily gathered together in the Palazzo
dei Musei where the remaining treasures of the Estense are housed.[2]
I think the last of the family may have sold some of the artwork to
British and American millionaires in the nineteenth century, but
there are still lots of paintings, armor, ceramics, and archaeological
treasure troves in Modena. We spent a number of happy hours in
the various museums and innocently asked where we could see the

---

[2] We wondered how the Este collection got from Ferrara to Modena. The family had
some ups and downs after the lovely daughters of Duke Ercole I made their spectacular
marriages. By 1598, an illegitimate great-grandson of Lucrezia Borgia and Alfonso Este
became duke. The pope refused to recognize him, and, having at the time a sizable army,
took control of Ferrara. As usual, the emperor was on the outs with the papacy, and made
the young man Duke of Modena. His name was Cesare, and he moved the entire family
into the new duchy, where they stayed up to the time of the American Civil War. It took
something like six hundred baggage wains to carry the artwork and furniture to their
new castle. Amazingly, their secretaries and notaries managed to defy the old adage that
"two moves are as good as a fire," and kept the entire archive of political negotiations,
kitchen bills, military treaties, social correspondence, and sisterly letters together, and it
still exists either in Ferrara or Modena.

"Borso d'Este," not knowing whether it was a pocketbook or an early form of stock exchange.[3] A most obliging librarian got out a bunch of keys and led us through the study rooms of a contemporary library to a showcase that contained the most marvelous manuscript we have ever seen. This Bible, for such it turned out to be, was made in the late fifteenth century, just as printing was beginning to replace illuminated manuscripts, if indeed the "Borso" is really the product of hand lettering. The brilliant execution of the text seems almost too regular to have come from the pen of a scribe. Of one thing there is no doubt: the illuminations done by Taddeo Crivelli are wonderworks of the illuminator's art. Saints, dragons, seashells, flowers, and abstract designs frame each page. Huge uncial initials on each chapter or paragraph are decorated with gilded backgrounds, fantastic arabesques, paisley shapes, and flowers. The librarian was proud to show it off.

Later, while exploring the church of San Pietro, we were beckoned by a young verger to view the paintings in the sacristy, the room in which the priests put on their vestments before mass or other ceremonies. The process of vesting is surrounded by ceremony and prayer, especially in the case of bishops who even have special prayers for putting on their white shoes. To keep the good padres' minds on track, vestries are required to have a crucifix on display, and in many cases the entire room is lavishly decorated with religious art. In some churches the greatest paintings were thus hidden away in this private location; perhaps not a bad idea if they served to get the reverend cranked up for a good homily.

The verger told us there would be a short organ recital in a few minutes, and that the organ dated from 1525. He gave us plenty of

---

[3] I discovered later that Borso d'Este was a person, the member of the family who commissioned the Schifanoia palace in Ferrara as well as a famous Bible.

time in the sacristy, and when we returned to the church, he locked
the door behind us and then went to the nave to welcome a pair of
young visitors who seemed to be waiting for him. There were embraces,
greetings, and a moment's happy talk in rapid Italian. He then switched
on some lights that showed off a magnificent organ front above our
heads and disappeared up a stair to the tracker keyboard, hidden in the
gallery of the instrument. He had not told us that he was the organist
as well as the verger, and probably sexton as well. The mighty old
pipes made the building echo with J. S. Bach for about three-quarters
of an hour. We and the young couple were his only audience. He
spoke excellent English, played very well indeed, and collected CDs
of Anthony Newman. We told him that we would introduce him if
he ever got to the United States, and, attempting to feel a little like
Renaissance patrons of a young artist, forced him to accept a few
thousand lira notes to get him started on saving for the airfare.

　　We had a full day of museums, music, and walking about
the center of the town. We dined in the second-floor trattoria,
Da Enzo, run by the same family that owned the hotel and not
far from the success of the night before. We finally abandoned all
that my cardiologist recommended and ordered the *bollito misto*
we had been observing in Emilian restaurants for some time. The
selections included tongue, *zampone*, beef, capon, calves' head, and
cotechino sausage. I commanded a bottle of *lambrusco*, the light, fizzy
red wine that is requisite with such fare. Although my wife found
it less enchanting, I felt that it cut through the weight of the meat
with great success. With all the condiments it was not exactly a light
supper, but then, think of the educational experience.

　　If the food of Emilia-Romagna is a trifle rich at times (I mean,
these people sometimes put butter on their thinly sliced ham!), the
drink provided is light. These days it's usually easy to find Northern

Italian wines in the U.S., and although we all know Chianti and
Soave, even these will offer some pleasant novelty when tasted in
their home court. White wines like Est!Est!Est!, Prosecco, Orvieto,
Verdicchio, and Pinot Grigio may be new experiences for you. We
combined our practice of drinking mostly white wine (saving the
reds like Valpolicella for game and Bolognese Ragù) with the Italian
custom of having wine with at least two of the three meals of the
day. But Italians are moderate in the amount of wine they drink at
any one time. We adopted their pattern of ordering a half-liter of
acqua minerale along with a half-liter of the house white at lunch.
The local wines were almost always delightful and a great bargain.
We occasionally asked a nice waiter to pick out a bottle for us,
giving him a price range to work from. This is how we discovered
Est!Est!Est!, a semi-*secco* of Tuscany.[4] Even small restaurants stock
several brands of mineral water, with San Pellegrino being perhaps
the most popular. We usually took whatever the house offered; they
all seemed very good to us. We liked the sparkling variety (*gasata*),
but you can also have it without bubbles (*normale*) if you wish.

Getting back late to the Libertà, we switched on the television
to check on the world as we got ready for bed. The scene was
familiar, from an old movie that at first I did not recognize. And
then we realized it was from *Amarcord*, Fellini's gentle and most

---

[4] The name comes from a story of the eleventh century. The Cardinal Archbishop
of Augsburg was going to Rome, surely for some serious ecclesiastical reason. He sent
his steward ahead to reconnoiter the inns along the way, marking those with good wine
in chalk with *Est!* (It Is!). When the bishop got to Montefiascone, near Viterbo but well
short of Rome, he came upon an inn marked with the word three times, followed by a
series of exclamation marks. Entering, he discovered his servant, quite unconscious with
a blissful smile on his face. Impressed, the Bishop called for a stoup of the best vintage.
He drank so much that he too passed out, but, unfortunately never came to and was
buried in the village of Montefiascone, where he still lies. Both the wine and its source
are still there too, the temporary chalk designation having been made the permanent
name of the inn as well as the vintage.

autobiographical masterpiece of the 1960s. We knew at once that he must have died, and thought that a few clips of his films were being used to illustrate the newscast. But no, the scenes went on until it all reeled again before us: Uncle Matthew being coaxed down from the tree by the midget nun; the woman news vendor with the enormous bosom and the adolescent boy; the lovers separated by the heaped-up walls of snow which were shoveled from the paths in the cathedral square. All the other programming had been canceled to air it as a memorial to Fellini. For the next several days the newspapers and the TV were largely devoted to mourning the loss of *nostro* Federico. All of the magazines we saw on the airplane flying home several weeks later devoted most of their space to him. He was a friendly hero to all Italians, a beloved relative who understood them, and of whom they could be justly proud. Luciano Pavarotti's pontifical 2007 funeral in Modena was also an example of the reverence Italians pay to their artists.

We left Modena without visiting either of the hot rod automobile factories or seeing the Ferrari museum of bright red cars. But we loved this town; even the quality of hotel was superior to its rating. We found that like the cars, everything—tenors, art, music, film, history, food—all are world-class in Modena.

XII

RAVENNA
Christianity and Civilization in a Dark Age

Ravenna today seems to be an ordinary place with extraordinary things in it. The old town is small and ringed by petrochemical factories. It is far surpassed in population by the beach towns a dozen miles to the east, where the sea went when it deserted this late Roman city and withdrew.

The shifting sands of this part of the Adriatic were the cause of both the rise and decline of Ravenna. The town was naturally protected by impassible swamps when Rome began to look less secure from both the voracious crowds within the city and the surging barbarians to the north. As a result, later emperors (most of whom had only a shaky grasp on the purple) began to spend more and more time at what must originally have been a kind of imperial resort. Finally, Honorius, after trying Milan as a capital and discovering he was even more in the path of visiting barbarians, moved the whole executive structure of government to Ravenna in 404, leaving what was left of the Senate behind to shift for itself. That was just about in the nick of time, since Alaric took Rome in 410.[1] Less than a century later, the Ostrogoths were lords of the Empire, and they used Ravenna as their capital.

But between the mid-fifth and sixth centuries, Honorius's sister, Galla Placidia, and the later Gothic king Theodoric, gave their minds and treasure to things of the spirit. This otherworldly Christianity was somewhat divided between Arian and Orthodox communions but unified by the most amazing works of mosaic to be found anywhere in the world.

There are two baptistries in Ravenna: one orthodox at the cathedral, and the other freestanding, known as the Arian Baptistery. An oversimplified differentiation between these two types of Christianity goes roughly this way: Arians (who were trying to use human reason to relate what they believed of Jesus to what they believed of God) felt that while Christ was unique, he was not eternal since he was begotten of God the Father. The difference between *genetos*, "made," and *gennetos*, "begotten," is frightfully important even though recorded by a single doubled letter and perhaps hard to hear at all in declamation. Most of the "we believe this, but not that" sort of definition in the early stanzas of the Nicene Creed come from the fathers attempting to settle this sort of thing back around 325 when the Emperor Constantine forced

---

[1] Alaric has gotten bad press through the years, some of it undeserved. He had been an officer in the Roman Army and was a Christian. The Roman army was full of hired Goths, the emperor was not exactly a square shooter, and when Alaric changed sides, lots of the army came with him. As a sacker of cities he did a mild job on Rome, not a patch on the real sack that took place when the Christian Constable of Bourbon, part of the entourage of the H.R. Emperor Charles V, brought down an army of mercenaries from virtually every country north of the Alps. He died of a crossbow bolt that Benvenuto Cellini claimed to have fired. The year was 1527. There being no orders from the distant German emperor, and no one in charge of the army, the soldiers, having taken the city, settled down to ten or eleven months of occupation during which murder and rape, arson, looting, and the torture of those who might have hidden valuables, set a record unsurpassed even by the Serbian militia men of our own time. Compared to the young fellows of Charles V's army, Alaric, and even Genseric—who did quite a job on the town in 455—could be considered minor-league Rome sackers.

the arguing factions on one of the issues to accept the term "consub-stantial," or *homoousios*, to define the relationship of the persons of the Trinity. All of this was very serious stuff in the fourth century, and it still is in some quarters today. Lots of heads were broken over questions of hypostatic union. What is known as the "filioque" clause helps to maintain the enmity of the Croats and the Serbs today.

By the time of the flowering of Ravenna, the Goths were still Arian and the somewhat more Roman population was orthodox. Some signs of this difference can be deduced from the great mosaics of the two baptistries. To western eyes, the orthodox apostles, the stuccoed figures of prophets, and the dove of the Holy Spirit have a familiar look to them. John the Baptist is pouring water from a handheld shell rather than pressing Christ down for total immersion, a detail some think is due to later restoration.

In the Arian baptistery, which was built by Theodoric fifty years later than the orthodox one (around the year 500), the image of Christ came as a shock to us. He is depicted in a brilliant mosaic as a young man, naked and beardless, standing half-submerged in the water, his Jewish masculinity clearly defined by circumcision. The Baptist's hand is on his shoulder, ready to submerge him. John looks a little anxious, obviously aware that this is no ordinary penitent, but a very human one nonetheless. The Spirit, in the form of a dove, pours "water from its beak upon the Lord's head," a detail which fits with the prophecy from the Book of Joel:

> *I will pour out my Spirit upon all flesh;*
> *And your sons and daughters shall prophesy,*
> *Your old men shall dream dreams,*
> *Your young men shall see visions; . . .*
> *In those days I will pour out my spirit.*

The colored tesserae of the mosaics are either stone, ceramic, or covered with gold leaf. They are as brilliant today as when they were assembled fifteen centuries ago.

Theodoric commissioned his own tomb before his death in 526. The building, reminiscent of Hadrian's tomb in miniature, is dodecahedral and made of Istrian stone from the far northern end of the Adriatic Sea near Trieste. It is vaulted over with a single, carved, dome-shaped slab more than thirty feet across and better than a yard thick. Presumably it was brought to the port of Classe on some raft of wonderfully ample proportion. The monolithic dome is estimated to weigh something like three hundred metric tons, so that raft must have been a monster. I wonder what propelled it? Theodoric's kingdom obviously did not lack either organization or inventiveness. His engineers still remembered the skills of the imperial centuries.

The older of the two Basilicas of St. Apollinaris is a few miles south of the center of the town in Classe. There was a near war over moving his relics to the other basilica in the town. He was the first bishop of Classe and this, his original resting place, is still used as a place of worship rather than as a museum. Even if its mosaics are less spectacular than the other St. A's, it is a wonderful building from the mid-sixth century. The bishop who ordered it built had the financial backing of Julian the Silversmith, referred to in a contemporary guidebook as "the mysterious and very rich Greek" who almost simultaneously was also paying for the building of Saint Vitalus's basilica back in town. If most of the Roman Empire was deep in the dark in the sixth century, a languidly bright and beautiful spot thrived at Ravenna.

The decoration of the great Basilica of Saint Apollinaris is Arian, having been commissioned by Theodoric in the early sixth century. Christ is once again depicted as young and unbearded, looking like a youthful Roman patrician, although he grows a beard and matures visibly as the sequence of New Testament scenes unfolds. Below the clerestory windows, the upper walls present a seemingly endless file of the blessed, robed in gold and white, and carrying palms in their hands. In that nave you can still feel the security of the rigidly ordered Byzantine civilization hanging on inside its walls, bemused by the theology and the artifice of the East. This is the time that Yeats imagined when he wrote

Once out of nature I shall never take
My bodily form from any natural thing
But such a form as Grecian goldsmiths make
Of hammered gold and gold enamelling

To keep a drowsy Emperor awake;
Or set upon a golden bough to sing
To lords and ladies of Byzantium
Of what is past, or passing, or to come.

While all the while the fierce and still destructive Langobards savaged the countryside to the west and prepared to breach the defenses of the town.

XIII

URBINO
The Renaissance Began in the Mountains

The hill town of Urbino rates a scant twelve-or fifteen-line entry in the five feet of shelf space that my encyclopedia occupies. Its name, however, crops up in Wikipedia and many other entries about the people, artists, and style of the Italian Renaissance. *Let's Go Italy* was less restrained: "If you only visit one town in Italy, make it Urbino."

Getting to Urbino takes a little planning. This is one of the towns we approached in a rented Fiat Panda, which had to be urged over some of the hills in a variety of lower gears. But even Urbino can be gotten to by public transportation by first taking a train down the Adriatic coast to Pesaro and then one of the ten daily buses that leave from the vicinity of the station. Alternatively, you might get a bus from Assisi and approach from the west. The trip up into the mountains is pretty, and you can see the high-turreted cutout of the little city above you against the sky shortly before you arrive. It is an uphill walk to the center of town, but there is said to be an elevator from the *parcheggio* where the buses stop that will take you most of the way. We drove around the base of the town twice searching for a way in. As a university town more than a commercial center, Urbino has a limited number of hotels, but the guidebooks speak well of the Albergo Italia and the Hotel San Giovanni. We stayed at the Bonconte.

Whenever we changed cities, we prevailed upon the desk clerk of our current hotel to make our reservation for two nights hence. This put the least strain on my beginning Italian and seemed to please the clerks. As we found with dinner reservations, the clerks assumed the role with flair and emphasis, usually in a loud voice and very rapid Italian with a sort of upper-class distinctness of speech. Some offered advice about which hotel we should book. One clerk made three calls to find us the sort of room we wanted. He didn't charge us for the calls, but was happy to accept a thousand-lira tip, more I think for the resultant esteem than for its value.

The famous Urbino of the later *quattrocento* is largely the work of Federico Montefeltro, successor to a family of strong men of the Marches who raised the county to the status of a duchy. He was the illegitimate son of Guidantonio, Count of Urbino, the Captain of the Papal Army, and of Elisabetta degli Accomanducci dei Conti di Petroio of Gubbio. His birth was kept a secret for two and a half years to spare the feelings of the countess, and also to protect the identity of his mother who was much under the age of consent at the time of her seduction. But the countess died in 1423, leaving Guidantonio with an infant heir who was soon killed by enemies of Urbino.

He moved swiftly to marry the pope's niece,[1] but that lady, however legitimate, remained childless. With his new wife's consent, the count then recognized the infant Federico as his proper heir. But

---

[1] Papal family relationships are often subject to some historical confusion from the fact that the word *nipote* can mean nephew, and *nipotina* can mean either "little niece" or "little granddaughter." Thus, the fault we term "nepotism" could mean appointing any of one's own progeny to a post, not just those of the official's siblings.

soon the new countess surprised everybody by becoming pregnant. The resulting possibility for confusion in the line of succession led Guidantonio to send young Federico off to be reared by a widowed lady relative who ruled Sant'Angelo in Vado and Marcatello. To seal the bargain, the little boy was betrothed to her daughter Gentile and thus became heir to that earldom. This was presumably enough of an honor and responsibility to keep him busy and out of competition with his little brother. When he was eleven, having lived in the home of his fiancée for eight years, Federico was used as a hostage to Venice by the pope, and later was shipped to the Gonzaga court in Mantua where he received the best available classical education. When he was sixteen, he finally returned to Gentile who was then twenty-one. They were married in Gubbio. Federico then set out on a brilliant military career. He won all his battles, sometimes by

Federico Montefeltro
Dux Urbino

amazing feats of derring-do. He scaled the overhanging Rock of San Leo to defeat the Malateste, and was made hereditary Earl of Massa Trabaria by the pope in 1443.

At his father's death, Federico's younger half-brother (the fully legitimate one) was declared Count of Urbino and then made a duke by the pope. He was slain in a conspiracy the following year. Federico rushed to the town and arrived during the tumult that followed the murder. He met with the local magnates and impressed everybody with his intelligence and forcefulness. Soon after, he was carried triumphantly to the church where he was proclaimed Count and Lord of Urbino. It took thirty years before the next of several popes, the numerically redundant Sixtus the Fifth, made him Duke of Urbino and Gonfalonier of the Holy Roman Church.

I have no record of his succession of wives, although the documents surely exist. He certainly acquired more than one. The blond lady in the paired portraits in the Uffizi, painted by Piero della Francesca, is not Gentile, but Battista Sforza of Milan, a lady of even more impressive monetary endowment. That painting shows off the famous divot in the bridge of Federico's nose. The blemish is prominent in all of his portraiture because he was always painted in profile, having lost his right eye in the same jousting accident that took out the chunk of nose.

Federico was perhaps the greatest of that remarkable class of Italian characters, the *condottiere*, captains of the mercenary armies that fought the wars of the time. Italy was largely urbanized in the fourteenth and fifteenth centuries, and even the rural populations surrounding the cities were not under the feudal obligation of homage to a lord, a system that provided an easy means of conscription of armies in transalpine Europe. Townspeople were free citizens, and, although they would build walls and defend them in their own interest, they could not be readily conscripted and sent to war in the field against a rival army. The city communes therefore hired small professional armies, contracting with a captain who would provide troops, men, horses, weapons, and military know-how. Federico was not only a master of this profession, but he also acquired a justified reputation for fulfilling his contracts in an age where the double cross was the norm and alliances usually had to be assured by an exchange of treasure and hostages. As a result of his reputation for straight shooting, he gained the wealth which, coupled with good taste, enabled him to hire men like Luciano Laurana as his architect and the likes of Piero della Francesca, Paolo Uccello, and Raphael's father, Giovanni Santi, as painters.

Federico ran a sort of military school for young noblemen from other parts of Europe and supposedly trained princes from as far away as England in the arts of war. Poets and philosophers were welcome at his court. Many years later, during the reign of the last duke of the line, Baldasarre Castiglione wrote a memorable description of this Italian Camelot in *The Book of the Courtier*, which served as a handbook of politics, manners, and diplomacy for the later Renaissance. The Montefeltro Palace also seems to have functioned as a postgraduate university, where pursuit of classical language and literature was illuminated by learned discussion, and

Federico Montefeltro of Urbino

contemporary artists were encouraged to practice painting and architecture. Some commentators have ventured the opinion that the Renaissance as an intellectual movement really began at Urbino.

What with all the climbing, we were happy to slide back down to the wall where we were put up at the friendly Hotel Bonconte in a pleasant room a little removed from the center of the *passeggiata* of the young and old in the Piazza della Repubblica. A half-hour *pisolino* rallied us for a return to the fray. In attempting to find our inn earlier in the day, we had driven to the summit and somehow passed through some stone posts, intended as a checkpoint turning traffic away, to find ourselves in the rear court of a restaurant called Pasta à Gogo. The proprietor was vastly amused by our ability to navigate the little Fiat through the supposedly interdicted streets at the top of the hill. He guided us on a route down to Via della Mura and was even more amused when I translated it as "Wall Street." The downhill course over the slates and cobbles was as breathless as the descent of a forty-meter Olympic ski jump, but the brakes held and we found the Bonconte at the bottom of the slope.

In spite of the outdated, faddish name, we found the dinner at Pasta à Gogo delicious and the friendly *proprietario* helpful and voluble. His selection of a special wine was only moderately pricey and a wonderful experience. We signed the guestbook and have received several Christmas and New Year's cards in the ensuing years. Walking back down the steeply sloping stones of the town late at night was an experience totally removed from home. Why we came.[2]

Before leaving Urbino, we discovered the dark side of both medieval and contemporary Europe in a fascinating and well-known

---

[2] Subsequent research on the Internet suggests that Pasta à Gogo is no more, but it's possible that only the name has been changed.

work of art. One of the most enigmatic paintings of the *quattrocento* is the set of six little panels from an altar predella by Paolo Uccello. They depict the story of "The Profanation of the Host." Guidebooks and commentators say the scenes show a guilty woman who sells a consecrated communion wafer to a Jewish merchant. For some inexplicable reason (did he *believe* it was true flesh?), he attempts to cook the host in a pan before his fireplace. It runs over with bright blood that seeps under the door of his house and attracts the attention of soldiers, who attack the door with crowbars and axes. The sacrament is restored to the tabernacle in a richly vested procession; the woman is taken out at night to be hanged; the merchant and all his family are burned at the stake, also under cover of darkness. Two pairs of angels and devils wrestle over the body of the woman which is laid out in some dignity in front of the altar.

It is worth noting that this tale of anti-Semitic guilt by reputation, and the summary lynching in the darkness, is positioned on an altar supporting the tabernacle, a pious embellishment to accentuate the holiness of the sacrament and to teach reverence for it. Was it based on some actual, horrible witch hunt in the ages before Uccello's own time? Who commissioned it? I like to think that the sympathetic depiction of the merchant is, like Shakespeare's Shylock, an example of the work of an artist who at least points out the ambiguity of human guilt, even if there is nothing he can do to deflect the near-universal disapprobation or blunt the popular choice of vengeance. Such voices are like that of Justice Blackmun speaking against capital punishment while a chorus of popular politicians cried out for more frequent use of the gas chamber, the electric chair, and the lethal needle.

The woeful face of the woman, gazing piteously upward with the rope already looped around her neck, could not have been done by a painter who did not have compassion for the convicted. I also see nothing in any of the scenes that Uccello intended the merchant to be recognized as a Jew. He has no beard or costume detail that might represent him as such. The painting above his hearth shows the profile of a black, a scorpion, and an *eight*-pointed star. I wonder who first designated the hapless merchant, the host buyer, as a Jew?

The tiny figures on the little panels are brilliant and heartbreaking. Whatever enlightenment has occurred since the *quattrocento*, assignment of Semitic guilt seems still to be present in the modern attribution of unredeemable sin to the religion of the profaner and his wife and children. How many generations are still to be reared on such tales?

XIV

THE BOYS OF THE RENAISSANCE
Clearly Related to Those of Today

Once, while leafing through the glossy pages of a guidebook cataloging most of the contents of the Uffizi, it struck me with some surprise that the lavish exploration of human circumstance I was looking at was biased by both sex and age. There were many beautiful women of various stages of maturity, lots of babies and toddlers, and a number of children. There were old men and gods in the form of patriarchs, mature men as warriors, dukes, and knights. There are naked boys in the form of cupids and *putti* who are fat little blobs of masculinity flying around Tiepolo's ceilings. But there are relatively few older boys, young fellows in the physical flowering of their late teens or early twenties. Caravaggio painted early teenagers, at least one of whom he obviously liked, but Adam appears to have been created by God as a postadolescent man of some maturity. He usually looks to be in his early to mid-thirties as represented by most Renaissance artists.

Only a few—Titian, Pontormo, and his disciple Bronzino, in particular—lavished much of their talent and attention on depictions of the immediately postpubescent male. Bronzino's models are as much with us today in modern Italy as are the descendants of the girls

who posed for Bellini and Raphael. (Finding a real Giorgione walking
with her boyfriend in Milan or Rome is much rarer.) Pontormo's
Halberdier is a good example of the type rarely depicted by others:
the painting abounds in phallic symbols of sword pommel and staff,
although no halberd is evident. The young man's glance reveals an
interior chemistry composed of about equal parts of testosterone
and narcissism.

PONTORMO — *Halberdier* — 1527

Pontormo's paintings emphasize the gallant, daring self-
admiration of the nineteen-year-old. Bronzino's youths are more
intensely in need of relief, and look meltingly in the direction of
the nearest female who might be persuaded to help them attain it.
Both are in an obviously perpetual state of readiness for copulation
for most of their waking (or sleeping) hours. The only surcease
for this continuing state of rigidity would seem to be in relatively

brief postcoital intervals. Their lives are thus a continuing quest for consummation wherever it might be found.

Titian's *Young Man in the Red Cap* is now in New York at the Frick Collection. But his double, with the same deep brown, painfully passion-filled eyes, sits at the little tables in café bars, in Venice or Verona, reaching across the table to hold both of the hands of some ravishing teenaged beauty that he contemplates with wordless desire. The melting gaze has a sort of 750-watt microwave quality that will surely turn the young lady's heart and resolution to the viscosity of a *crema caramella* after a few minutes' exposure.

I saw a perfect modern example of Pontormo's young man-at-arms strolling the Milanese galleria with his companion, one arm circling her waist, his hand lodged in the far-side rear hip pocket of her tight blue jeans, where it was securely held in a permanent and possessive caress of her buttocks. His imperious stare at the rest of the world reflected great pride in the acquisition of the franchise he thus displayed.

Sculpture of young men is another matter. Oddly, the nude male is far more chaste than the clothed models of the paintings. The dreamy gaze of Michelangelo's *David* has nothing of desire in it. The various Apollos are all quite apollonian, and Mercury, flashy and speedy as he may be, is bent on obediently delivering the messages of the gods rather than his own *billets-doux*.

Perhaps the sexless quality of the male nudes of the Renaissance comes from the association of all other young male nakedness with the two most often depicted during the period: the deposition of the dead Christ and the arrow-riddled body of the standing Saint Sebastian. Those flaccid bodies are archetypes of Italian art. Any hint of the turgid sexuality of the real young male is close to sacrilege. If the eyes of the model are to convey any suggestion of that perpetually burning, tormented search for a companion in detumescence, the body must be covered up by the luxurious raiment of the young courtier or soldier. In any case, it must be unmistakably removed from any similarity to the stripped bodies of Sebastian or Jesus.

Even aside from outright sexuality, affection among contemporary Italian males is displayed differently from the way Americans are used to. Once at lunch in a pizzeria in a small Italian town, we vicariously enjoyed a birthday party for a young man in his twenties. There was much laughter and teasing over the glasses of wine and whipped-cream-covered desserts. The birthday boy then made a short speech and thanked all of the guests by making the full circuit of the table, kissing everyone on both cheeks, men and women alike. Watching high school students setting off to class reveals a similar ease with physical affection that American kids could never emulate. As the time to enter the building approached, the whole group said farewell for the next few hours with many hugs and kisses on both cheeks, boys with girls, girls with girls, and boys with boys. It also occurred to me that young American males would be horrified to be seen in public with the book-filled backpacks that their Italian counterparts strapped on. The design of the rucksacks was the same, but the boys in Italy favored bags made of pink, lavender, and spring-green nylon canvas.

XV

CORTONA
The Very Acme of the Hill Town

I can't remember why we determined to visit Cortona. It was on the best route coming back north to Siena after our stop at Urbino, but it wasn't given much space in the guidebooks. They all made mention of it, and the few lines in Michelin were intriguing. We had never heard of it but decided to give it a try.

The town roosts on top of an ancient hill in an upland plain between the watersheds of the Arno and the Tiber. It sits off the left shoulder of the Apennines, within sight of the great bowl of Lake Trasimeno to its south. The lake area attracts vacationers today. Once, more than two thousand years ago, it was the site of one of the major victories of the then seemingly invincible Carthaginians under Hannibal, who had come from Africa through the snowy high-altitude passes of the Alps and descended into Italy. He took the plain of the Po and ravaged his way down the river valleys to this point. It was here that the Romans led by Flaminius stood to wage battle. The augury of swarms of bees settling on the eagles of the Roman standards should have warned them that the day would not go well. Even more significant was the lakeside mist that rose from the osiers and fens. It disguised the presence of Hannibal's cavalry, which was unnoticed in the early fighting and then fell upon the Roman rear. The result was devastating. Rome itself seemed destined to be taken when its army was defeated even more decisively in the subsequent slaughter farther south in Apulia, at Cannae.

Roman and Carthaginian commentators felt that Hannibal could have destroyed the city on the Tiber within the week if "he had known as well how to use his victory as how to gain it."[1] But Hannibal rested his army still farther south at Capua, where his soldiers "grew soft in luxury" while the Romans made new arms, freed slaves to swell their shattered army, and prepared for his advance. The Roman commander Fabius gave his name to the gradual approach to solving political or social affairs by delaying any decisive conflict.

Hannibal stayed in southern Italy for fifteen years, but he never conquered Rome even though he never lost a battle. The Romans jabbed at his supply lines, and eventually Scipio invaded Africa to threaten Carthage itself. Hannibal then packed up his diminished troops and went home.

The wealth of precise information we have about these bloody years (218 to 202 BC), and our total ignorance of equally horrible and more decisive events that occurred six or eight centuries later in the same part of the world, makes the period before and after the Roman zenith seem even more obscure by contrast. Who swam or fished in Lake Trasimeno after the soldiers' bodies rotted away? Few were around to bury them.

In Cortona we urged the little car up steep streets to the Piazza della Repubblica, and we were able to look down at the Umbrian plain and the distant prospect of the lake from our pleasant room in the Hotel San Michele. But later we learned that we had hardly scaled

[1] Adherbal, the son of Bomilcar, evidently wrote this, although who saved his writing from the later destruction of Carthage I do not know.

the height of Cortona. Walking ever upward on the following day, we reached the Etruscan walls, huge sandstone blocks whose smoothly fitting irregular shapes remind me of the Inca stonework in Peru.

Cortona was first settled by the Umbrians, whoever they were, even before the Etruscans fortified it. It certainly does give the impression of being a very old town, although one of its prettier buildings is a nineteenth-century Romanesque church on the flank of the hill below the town, a shrine to St. Margaret of Cortona who died in 1297, just before the Renaissance broke upon the town.[2]

Cortona, never large, has room for only 20,000 people on top of the hill today, and I doubt that it has ever been larger. It was the home of Luca Signorelli, whose fantastic crowds of naked figures in murals of the Last Judgment in Orvieto were a prefiguring of Michelangelo's work. His paintings are in the Diocesan Museum. In this collection is yet another Annunciation, this one by Fra Angelico, that my wife ranks at the top of the genre in all of Italy.

Another museum is the Etruscan Academy, a modern continuation of an eighteenth-century intellectual club that numbered Voltaire among its early members. The Etruscans have always exercised a strong pull on the European imagination, both because they were the greatest competition for the early Romans and because

---

[2] Margaret is styled a "concubine" in the terminology of the church, although we might classify her as more of a mistress today. At least she doesn't seem to have been a professional lover, and if she had been, the more likely designation would have been "courtesan." Her iconography is of a pretty young woman being led by her dog, who tugs her along by a fold of her skirt held in his mouth toward the discovery of what is either the corpse of her lover or a more generalized *memento mori* in the form of a skeleton, presumably the incident that led to the reform of her life. Most female saints are classified as virgins, martyrs, widows, and sometimes even queens. Obviously belonging to none of these designations, Margaret is venerated as a penitent, a truly honorable kind of saint when you consider that it is also the title given Mary Magdalen. The attractive church is also known as the Church of Santa Maria del Calcinaio—"Holy Mary of the Lime Pits," for the local plaster deposits. It is the cover illustration of this book by Virginia Wright Frierson.

we know so very little about them. Their language is still virtually unreadable, their customs mysterious, and their origins unknown. Some think they may have come from Asia Minor. A prime example of their art in the Academy in Cortona is a circular chandelier of sixteen oil-burning lamps ringed with bacchantes pursued by lascivious fauns. It was turned up by a farmer's plow not very long ago. The remnants of the Etruscans are everywhere in Cortona.

Beyond the artistic and historic attractions of the town, Cortona is just a very nice place to be. The younger kids kicking a soccer ball around the piazza were a sort of counterpoint to the teenage girls strolling arm-linked in twos and threes, happy to be admired by the young men who stood on the corners watching the girls. The extreme climb and descent necessary for getting about the town have produced a crop of younger women with very good legs and older ones who would appear to have a touch of arthritis from the dogged, inevitable way they climb the steep streets. But people of all ages in Cortona seem to take appropriate enjoyment from being who they are, at any age.

The town is interested in things like the price of beef cattle on the hoof, the quality of this year's olive oil harvest, and the length of the season for maturing the grapes from the acres of vineyards that mantle the neighboring hills about the town. The colors of the countryside are deep ruddy brown of Umbrian soil and the silver-green of the olive trees that are everywhere about.

We found one restaurant that had good food but an overly pretentious way about it. On our second night we located the Trattoria Grotta, where the host was gracious and enthusiastic, the *vitella piccate* pounded to the thinness of lily petals, and the new season's asparagus an adventure still unforgotten. The town is well known for its good food and is the only place I have ever heard of that celebrates the feast of the Assumption of Mary (August 15) with a Beefsteak Festival. Cortona has long been a refuge for artists and writers, from Boston's Henry James to North Carolina's Virginia Wright-Frierson, who painted there and produced the grand cover scene of this book. It is off the main roads and has no railroad station, but its lofty mountaintop is bounded by spectacular views of Umbria and Tuscany from every window.

XVI

FIRENZE
The Full Bloom of the Renaissance with the Motorini at Full Bore

Despite the confusing series of impressions Firenze made on us when we first arrived, the meaning of it all became clear when we considered the source of the startling contrasts. It is a city of beauty and dirt, a jarring juxtaposition of powerful ancient structures and roaring modern motor vehicles, a place of Tuscan sunshine and Los Angeles smog. For Florence is about money, and it always has been. Money both produced and now defiles its beauty.

One of the town's earliest great municipal boasts is that this little city, which is even today only little more than the size of Bridgeport, Connecticut, undertook seven hundred years ago to build the largest cathedral in the world. They named it for Saint Mary of the Flowers and constructed the greatest part of it in less than twenty years, although it took over another century to close in its crossing with the largest dome attempted since the Romans roofed the Pantheon. No vengeful deity struck them down for their pride. They financed the project not on the resources of a continental empire, but from the money they made in wool, dyeing, and leather. They only lost the dome-span-and-altitude title several hundred years later when the popes built St. Peter's by tapping the wealth of all of North Europe from the sale of indulgences to those in terror of the punishment due to their manifest sinfulness. And, of course, although Rome seems an appropriate place for such a wonder, the popes were chastised for their ambition a few years after their dome was built by the outbreak of the Reformation.

But Rome is about power, whereas Florence is about money, and money can buy great art if the artists are given their freedom, while power cannot command art to serve it. Artists are notorious for subverting the power of absolute rulers, temporal as well as spiritual. I think this is why some Roman religious art looks theologically rebellious, even cynical. Artists will work quite honestly for an honest wage, but not at the absolute command of some ruler. This is why so much of the "Post Office Art" of the WPA is quite wonderful, while the later mural production of the Soviet Union is so dreadful.

Arriving in Florence on a spring holiday weekend, and at short notice, we found many of the choice bargains were jammed full of vacationing Italians. We ended up at the Royal, a nice small-sized hotel only a few lira over our usual budget and reputed to be "a ten-minute walk north of the duomo." We settled in for a most civilized tea in a conservatory, which opened onto an enclosed garden, and fortified ourselves for a preliminary foray into the art district. Here the other side of Florentine prosperity showed itself. The streets were narrow and innocent of sidewalks. The roaring of cars and the buzzing of *motorini* gave reasonable warning of their approach from behind, but there was often no place to hide from the simultaneous approach of another smoke-belching machine coming from the front. The pilots of these two- and four-wheeled pursuit ships were always in a blinding rush to get to something

or other and made it a point of honor to give no quarter in the
contest to be there, wherever, first.

Even in the roundabout of the cathedral and the baptistery, the
whirligig of vehicles, some bright, some battered, continues unabated,
giving an ironic twist to the nursery rhyme that kept coming around
in my head:

> Giro, girotondo
> Come è bell' il mondo![1]

Although I try to keep the image of the lavish distribution
of internal combustion engines from dominating my memory of
Florence, I think that oft-repeated walk into the oldest part of town
during my first visit in the 1990s scarred my sensibility. The peace of
central Ferrara and the almost eerie silence of Venice came to mind
as alternatives to the noisy pursuit of gain that propelled the never-
ending flow of cars, Vespas, and motorcycles around and around the
baptistery, campanile, and cathedral. In fairness, Firenze has made
progress in rerouting some of the traffic in subsequent years, and this
area has now been designated a traffic-free zone.

Florence is, like Rome, impossible to catalog without a whole
book devoted to it. Thanks mostly to the Medici, it houses the greatest
collections of art in the world, and being in Florence, the Florentines
charge the most for viewings: almost €10 for the Uffizi, and slightly
less for the other museums. It's not that they're not worth it; they
surely are. But by the time you have spent a full day among three or
four, several of which are not large, it is easy to drop well over €50

---

[1] Roughly translated, and to the tune of "Ring around the rosie / How the world
is lovely!"

just getting in and out of the galleries. It discourages repeat visits and drop-ins. But never mind; eat the best food in Modena and Bologna, where the museums are cheap, and dine simply in Florence where Botticelli reigns supreme. Sandro Botticelli is surely one of the reasons to come to Italy in the first place.[2]

From among many great paintings, there are two absolutely stupendous nudes in the Uffizi: Titian's *Venus of Urbino* and Botticelli's *Birth of Venus*. The former would cause an uproar among the political and religious right if it were shown on early evening television in the United States. The latter presents an equally naked mythological beauty so pure that she could be exhibited in the refectory of a seminary. Less than sixty years of time separates these two beautiful women, but an ocean of differentiated taste and sensibility lies between.

The most famous and often-reproduced lady on the shell[3] is only one of Botticelli's paintings here. I grew up in a house where a good, large-scale print of the *Madonna of the Magnificat* hung in a circular frame in the living room. Finally seeing the real thing, full-sized, about twice the dimension of the childhood memory, was an exciting moment. And then, of course, there is the companion piece to Venus, *la Primavera*.

We had made some preparation for visiting Florence by reading Vasari's *Lives of the Most Excellent Painters, Sculptors and Architects*

---

[2] He was on the Medici payroll for most of his life and gave full measure for their patronage. Almost thirty of his paintings are in the gallery that used to be their "office" building, the Uffizi. If one could rank a few of them as less successful than others, it could only be in comparison to the exaltation of his most wonderful works. Any one of his paintings would qualify as the *capolavoro* of nearly any other painter.

[3] And she was indeed a lady—sort of. She was Simonetta Catteneo, the wife of Marco Vespucci, brother of the well-traveled Amerigo, for whom our country is named. Simonetta was also the beloved of Giuliano de' Medici, who paid Botticelli's salary. Giuliano also shows up as Mercury in the springtime painting, and with his brother as an attendant angel in the round *Madonna of the Magnificat*.

years before, but we could have done a lot more research to our
profit. Vasari's accounts are brief, but they give a feeling for life in
Renaissance Florence. Of course, it takes more than one trip to get to
know it. Seeing the whole richness of the Florentine art collections at
one time was more than I could handle. The mix of art, architecture,
and the tragedies and triumphs of human life are so rich that you
must abandon yourself to seeing it a little at a time; then, you must
go home and learn something about it if you are to come away with
anything but a sensation of surfeit from the experience.

During a later visit to Florence, we explored the city by
strolling down the Por San'Maria to the Ponte Vecchio and back
through the traffic of people of all nations enjoying the city.
Around the corner to the northeast on the proper side is one of
the most agreeable places in which we have stayed in Italy. The
Hotel Porta Rossa is on the street of the same name and claims to
be the oldest hotel in town. A good deal of it is descended from the
Palazzo Torrigiani, built back in the 1300s. A lot of remodeling and
modernization went on in the nineteenth century, and the hotel
was totally renovated in 2008.

We were given an enormous room on an upper floor that was
approached by alternating flights of stairs and modern elevators.
Although we were only on the third floor (fourth by our way of
counting), the ceiling heights are so great that we were able to look
out above the level of most of the multistoried buildings across the
way. At $105 a night (*colazione incluso*)—perhaps a bit more like
125 euro now, what with a weak dollar and a strong euro—it was
at the time a touch high on our fiscal thermometer, but it was in a
near perfect location in central Florence near the Via Tornabuoni,
where fashionable shops of the likes of Gucci, Cartier, and other

even less affordable things are clustered. The lobby of the hotel was full of overstuffed leather chairs and sofas and contained a clubby sort of bar; a nice place to meet people and get in out of the art for a few moments' recuperation.

Florence is of Roman origin and thus young among Italian cities. Its hilltop satellite, Fiesole, is much older, having been an Etruscan town and later a far more important Roman site than what was to become the queen city of Tuscany in the valley of the River Arno, which both embraces and threatens it. There is virtually no reference to Florentia in the Roman records, and the traces of its city walls show it to have been almost insignificantly small. But its streets were laid out Roman fashion, at right angles, and the pattern still exists in the center of the town, south of the duomo and north of the Via Porta Rossa. These streets are still oriented to the compass points rather than to the banks of the Arno, giving an otherwise illogical twist to the main thoroughfares of Florence. Today a tourist can see only the pattern of the streets to suggest the Roman town except for a few traces in the excavations under the duomo and in the capitals of a few columns in the monastery of San Miniato on the hill across the river, where the best view is.

Florence, whose Latin name would seem to mean "flourishing" rather than "flowery," was a place of manufacture of woolen cloth and metalwork from its earliest years. It must have been a pleasant little city in the time of the Caesars, still small enough to have been surrounded by fields and olive orchards close to town. The Arno transported its commerce down to the sea at Pisa and Livorno, towns that the Florentines took over more than a thousand years later in the late Middle Ages. The Via Cassia, one of the straight military roads, connected it with the capital at Rome. But despite these

connections to the larger world of the Roman Empire, the little
city eventually underwent a more rapid and complete contraction
than the larger cities during the rough times of the Dark Ages. Yet
its decline was not sudden. One of the last real successes of the
great western Roman armies took place here when Stilicho, their
only capable commander, defeated a sizable army of Ostrogoths
between Florence and Fiesole in 405. But Stilicho was betrayed by
the courtiers of a do-nothing emperor, Honorius, and eventually
was beheaded in Ravenna a few years later. The emperor stayed
in Ravenna and the Goths, under Alaric, went on to sack Rome
in 410. No emperor ever returned to Rome or to Florence, and
several generations later, the boy emperor Romulus Augustulus
was deposed from his refuge at Ravenna in 476, bringing an end
to the western empire and leaving the country to Odoacer,[4] the
first of the Gothic kings who governed most of Italy for the next
generation or two. Then there were Huns and eventually, at the
end of the sixth century, the Langobards. In all it took less than two
centuries to undo that brilliant, cruel, and in many ways corrupt
civilization of Rome. But it has bulked large in the memory of
Europe ever since.

These events redistributed the population of Europe, but
reduced the population of Florence from perhaps ten thousand to
as little as a thousand people by the year 600. Still, there was some
reorganization going on. The city became Christian, and a large
church dedicated to the almost unknown St. Reparata was built on
the site of a Roman building of considerable size. Its foundations

---

[4] Odoacer had a certain respect for the forms of the empire, and put the emperor
into forced retirement in a villa near Naples with a pension of 6,000 golden soldi. Nobody
seems to know what happened to him when (or even if) he grew up.

and the outline of its walls and apses are still there in the crypt of the duomo. We have several times made the exciting and slightly spooky descent in both space and time, walking around in the holy gloom among foundation stones of the first and sixth centuries with the unimaginable weight of the fourteenth-century structure balanced above us on huge masonry piers. The sheer scale of the "modern" cathedral (now more than seven hundred years old) gave me a sense of awe at the ability of the Renaissance architects and engineers. How did they raise those stones so far? Probably with huge man-powered squirrel-cage wheels that reeled in the hand-twisted ropes and pulleys and lifted the blocks of limestone and the baskets of bricks.

Later, when Filippo Brunelleschi took over as *capomaestro* of construction of the dome, he invented an ox-powered hoist with wooden gears and cogs that transmitted the animal power at ground level to the site of the work, eventually almost 400 feet above.

But in the time before the building of the great cathedral, there are practically no records of the sixth, seventh, and eighth centuries. We have no narrative of killer floods like the one that washed down the Arno and drowned the town in 1966, although Florence probably experienced more than one.[5] And yet, during those obscure years of the Dark Age, Florence began to produce well-woven and colorfully dyed cloth, as well as fiery preachers who attempted to purge the citizens of their sins and the church of its corruption, as well as money changers who kept records of credit. All three of these commodities made the town almost as famous as the international

---

[5] The original Ponte Vecchio was carried away by one of these riparian tidal waves in 1333. The Val d'Arno is really a floodplain that will be inundated at least once every century.

bankers and artists of later centuries. Merchants, churchmen, and the nobility exchanged places of authority many times, often repeating the pattern of favoring the Holy Roman Emperors or the Pope. The Ghibelline and Guelph parties sided in this way and battled through the ages. Ghibellines usually backed the Holy Roman Emperor who was most usually German. Members of the Guelph party stuck by the pope (generally Italian), but not always too loyally. Later this party divided itself into Blacks and Whites just to keep the savage rivalry going for a few more generations.

Florence was never democratically governed until modern times, but during an extended period of the eleventh and twelfth centuries, the power of pope, emperor, or nobility was subverted, and, as in some other cities, a commune was established. Many of these cities were governed by a council of eight or ten leaders of commercial guilds or other outstanding citizens. But the citizens were too often swayed by the popularity of the strong man, priest, or financier for a constitutional council or the representatives of the guilds to manage for long. Earlier, for a wonderful moment at the end of the eleventh century, the whole of Tuscany was ruled by a woman, the remarkable Matilda, the Great Countess. Her father had been assassinated, her brother died of more or less natural causes, and her somewhat distasteful husband was done in by another assassin. She thus inherited an enormous fief and was powerful enough to invite both Pope Gregory VII and Emperor Henry IV to come for a stay at her castle at Canossa in the neighboring hills, where she mediated their dispute. We followed up on her career during a visit to Reggio, when we headed north after leaving Florence. She was responsible for moving the administrative center of Tuscany from Lucca to Florence, wore shining armor when reviewing her troops, and was eventually memorialized by a tomb in St. Peter's Basilica in Vatican City. By her era, Florence had become a prosperous, boisterous, crowded, and surely dirty city.

By the later Middle Ages, the explosive spirit and argumentativeness of the Florentines had become legendary. They picked quarrels among themselves and with neighboring towns, with Siena, Prato, and Pistoia, with the emperor and often with the pope. They won only about as often as they lost, but the city grew and was rebuilt; the citizens enlarged Matilda's walls, and produced still more leather, cloth, dyes, and spices. Franciscan and Dominican friars established their convents and preached conversion of heart to the quarrelsome and the bloody-minded. Once an argument over a plate of food at a dinner party led to a savage exchange with rapiers and a blood feud of revenge. Later, a wedding was arranged to bring the fierce enemy families together, but the groom married another girl, thereby insulting the honor of the family of the spurned bride. He was slaughtered as he emerged from the church; his body and his distraught bride were placed in a carriage with his bloodied head in her lap. The grisly spectacle was exhibited throughout the city along the route intended for the wedding procession. The ensuing vendetta divided the town along lines of the Guelph and Ghibelline partisanship and continued for many years.

Shakespearean characters like Tybalt, Mercutio, and the rest of the Veronese Montagues and Capulets would have been quite at home in the Florence of this period, joyfully ready to drive sword or stiletto into the ribs of any member of the opposing team at a moment's notice, all the while dressed in the latest extravagant fashion and wearing hats with brilliant plumes and bulging codpieces whose colors signified their loyalties. Calm and rational discourse was not the usual pattern of city life in the city of flowers. The young men seemed to spend their lives halfway between tears of desire and savage rage, rushing from love to murder with appalling briskness.[6]

Today, if you drive south through the tunnels of the Autostrada del Sol and emerge in the valley of the Arno, you can see the whole town at once, its center marked by Arnolfo da Cambio's great cathedral, Saint Mary of the Flowers. The city is still small enough to drive around both its center and its modern extensions in less than twenty minutes. It has a population of about half a million. It may have been half that size in the fourteenth century before the great plague of the Black Death took more than half its people. Yet in the two hundred years immediately following that disaster, it produced or sheltered the development of Cimabue, Duccio, Giotto, Brunelleschi, Donatello, Ghiberti, Ghirlandaio, Raphael, Leonardo da Vinci, Michelangelo, Fra Angelico, Michelozzo, Uccello, Fra Lippo Lippi and his son Filippino, Pontormo, Botticelli, and Bronzino. And then, of course, there was its famous exile, Dante Alighieri, who was banished from the city for rendering a judgment against his own faction while he served a two-month term as a magistrate in 1302. Boccaccio was in town in the mid-fourteenth century when he wrote the immensely popular *Decameron*, the collection of one hundred tales told by a group of young bloods who were refugees from the plague in a country house.

---

[6] Does it have to do with geography or the firm hand of an absolutist ruler that the humanism which marked the Renaissance developed early in a hill town such as Urbino under the patronage of a *Conditorre* such as Duke Federico Montefeltro, and not in Florence? The Platonic academy of Florence had to wait until Lorenzo de Medici was firmly in charge of the town and the petty, bloody competitions of the earlier part of the *quattrocento* had been pretty much suppressed. Perhaps the lingering flavor of violence that accompanied democratic rule accounts for the later Italians' enthusiasm for Mussolini, or perhaps even the popularity of Berlusconi, who made a political comeback after being jailed for corruption. But it doesn't do much good to speculate on the form and duration of power in Italy now. They seem to have found that government is largely irrelevant to prosperity and an orderly life.

Even though savage competition and divisiveness plagued the city until it quieted down for a bit during the disaster of the Black Death, neither internecine warfare nor the horror of the plague were able to choke off the fountain of artistic inventiveness that welled up in this city. Dante, Boccaccio, Arnolfo de Cambio, Cimabue, Giotto, and Duccio made their great contributions when these interior quarrels were raging. In spite of Dante's ejection from the city to perpetual exile, everyone who could read did read *The Divine Comedy*, and after his death the city pleaded with the powers of heaven and earth to get his remains back to place them in an honored tomb in Santa Croce. They failed; he is today interred in Ravenna.

The tit-for-tat battling continued as long as the republican commune flourished, and even into the time when the Medici family dominated the town. In 1478 the powerful Pazzi, a rival banking family, plotted against the Medici with the connivance of Pope Sixtus IV. The Medici bank had demurred at making an enormous loan to the pope, who wanted to buy the city of Forlì to make a duchy for his son. The Pazzi not only volunteered the financing but agreed to rub out the house on Medici in the bargain. Their plot involved stabbing young Giuliano de Medici and his older brother Lorenzo while all heads were bowed at the elevation of the sacrament at high mass in the cathedral. Guiliano died, but Lorenzo leapt over the communion rail and escaped into the sacristy where his supporters barricaded themselves until help arrived. The people rallied to his support. The conspirators were in turn quite horribly punished when their coup d'etat failed. The ringleaders were castrated before they were slowly strangled, hanging from the upper porticoes of the Palazzo Vecchio. Those that weren't killed outright were banished. The Pazzi women were forbidden to marry (although Lorenzo relented of this punishment some years later). The Pazzi arms were chiseled off the facades of the buildings the family had owned for years before they took to brandishing their swords at mass in the great cathedral. A few years earlier they had commissioned and paid for a family chapel in Santa Croce that still bears their name. It was designed by Filippo Brunelleschi, the greatest of all the Renaissance architects. The cool rationality and mathematical simplicity of Brunelleschi's design presents an amazing contrast to the unruly history of the family that hired him.

Many of the stories of the city are shockingly bloody and marked by passionate partisanship. Today it would seem that the Florentines are in peaceful agreement with everyone and happy to be the hosts of the thousands of tourists who come here in all seasons to admire their remarkable works of art and architecture.

And there are tourists and students in plenty. Wherever we have gone on our recent visits to Italy we have been surrounded by the young. In the post-Easter recess or during assigned spring field-tripping, Florence was awash in an ocean of teenagers, laughing, looking, holding hands, photographing, and licking their cones of *gelato*. At the crest of the gentle arch of the Ponte Vecchio we noted modestly clad couples a few years their elders embracing in the archways that face east up the river. The ardor they displayed was in some contrast with the leisurely pace of the single scullers on the Arno who passed beneath the bridge. All around them the younger tourists crowded about while ignoring the lovers' private time in the timeless place.

On one of our trips to Florence we stayed in the apartment of a philosophy student who rented out a large bedroom and bath in his rather palatial digs on the fourth floor of a modern apartment building. When he had *clienti* in his own place he moved in with his parents next door. We found this agreeable location on the Por'Sant

Maria through Caffelletto, the useful organization which arranges
bed-and-breakfast accommodations in private homes in Italy. Living
almost precisely halfway between the Piazza della Signoria and the
Ponte Vecchio gave us the sense of being natives of this wonderful
place. In fact, we were in the center of what had been the location of
the medieval guild of silk weavers some seven hundred years before.
Coming home, we would thread through the crowds of tourists
and enter the private door on the busy street with a patronizing
glance at the outlanders *(forestiere)* from all over Europe who were
wandering the center of Florence with guidebooks in hand. We
walked the famous streets in the traces of Cosimo de Medici and his
grandsons, Giuliano and Lorenzo. We were located at the crossroads
where the partisans of the Pazzi were apprehended and slaughtered

FIRENZE   S. MARIA dei FIORE   c. 1290-1490

by the vengeful supporters of the *palle d'oro,* the golden balls of the Medici escutcheon.

Most of Florence as we see it is still the city altered and redesigned in the century before the famous bankers and art patrons that succeeded Cosimo de Medici and his grandson the *Magnifico.* Arnolfo di Cambio was the architect of the thirteenth century who recut some streets through the medieval town and designed the principal buildings that defined its *piazze.* First was the Church of Santa Croce to the west of the center, which he remodeled extensively and gave its present facade. Later, in the area beside the ancient baptistery, he drew the foundation plan of the new cathedral on top of the original duomo, Santa Reparata. Here he planned the construction of the largest building in the world. It is a vast and somewhat gloomy space that is huge even by our standards today, but bears the most delicate name of all the churches in Italy: Santa Maria del Fiore, Saint Mary of the Flowers.

Arnolfo di Cambio designed the great church and directed its erection as far as the great void over the crossing. Then he died only six years into the project and left the other architects who followed him without a scrap of design for spanning the dome. It is doubtful if he knew how the task was to be accomplished. Work went on for a long time while the great octagonal drum that crowned the crossing was left roofless for want of a plan to span it.

It was a greater span than anyone had ever attempted and, since it started several hundred feet above the level of the street, it was impractical to rest the masonry of the cupola on temporary wooden staging until the completed arching could support itself by leaning, as it were, against itself from the opposite sides of the empty space. From that point on up to the lantern at the summit of the dome, its structure and balanced strength were created from the inspired designs of another and much younger man, the artist and engineering genius Filippo Brunelleschi.

When the youthful Filippo Brunelleschi had come in second in the famous competition for the bronze doors of the Florentine baptistery,[7] he traveled to Rome with his friend Donatello and saw for the first time the remains of the classical architecture of Rome. Only a few intact Roman buildings were left, but then as now, the domed Pantheon was one of them. It is hard for us to realize, in our age of swift travel and photography, how amazing the first view of a city only a few hundred kilometers away from home could be. Brunelleschi, who was also a skilled engineer, was staggered by what he found, and set to work to measure the ruins and to draw plans of what the ancient buildings must have been like. Later, when he returned to Florence, he offered to design the dome for Santa Maria del Fiore, but because he was still in his twenties, he suggested that architects from all over Europe be asked to compete for the job. It took a number of years for the guild masters to decide that he should have the commission unencumbered by the ideas of other designers. He insisted that he could construct the dome without a center scaffold to hold it up while under construction, although he didn't tell in advance how he would accomplish this feat. (Sky hooks?) The clear span of the opening was 132 feet,[8] and the windowed lantern at the top was designed to stand over 300 feet above the floor below.

---

[7] Lorenzo Ghiberti won the contest, possibly on the recommendation of Donatello and Brunelleschi himself. The trial panels and the winner's strongly three-dimensional reliefs can be seen just across the piazza from the cathedral.

[8] It could contain a baseball diamond with room for first- and third-base coaches' boxes.

At the time it was to be the tallest building in Italy. Brunelleschi's plan required the construction of a pair of concentric, octagonal-ribbed domes built of specially cast interlocking bricks that hooked each to each and held themselves together as the work progressed from the outer rim up to the center. As the heavy material piled up above, chains embedded in the masonry kept the bottom from spreading. The finished design we see today is entirely dictated by the functional requirements of getting it built. It is about as free of extraneous decoration as John Roebling's Brooklyn Bridge. The space between the shells is large enough to contain kitchens for preparing the masons' dinner at midday. In later years, Michelangelo and Christopher Wren designed spans of similar size for St. Peter's and St. Paul's. Both acknowledged their debt to Brunelleschi's daring engineering. Michelangelo said his design was the sister of the Florentine model, perhaps a little bigger but not more beautiful than the dome of Santa Maria del Fiore.

Older than the cathedral's dome is the *campanile*, or bell tower. It was designed by Giotto around 1334 when the construction began, and was finished a half-century after his death. Reliefs by Andrea Pisano and Luca della Robbia were added as the work went along, but the design of the vertical lines and panels is very much the work of the old master who created the chapel in Padua and the frescoes in the lower chapel at Assisi. It might seem odd to us that a painter such as Giotto should be a brilliant architect too, but that was really the case of all the artists of the Renaissance. There was no difference between the trade of a painter or a sculptor and an architect. Leonardo, Michelangelo, Brunelleschi, and many others were hired to design public buildings, fortresses, and churches on the recommendation of their excellence as painters or sculptors. It probably wasn't a bad system. One reason that it worked was that the actual construction was in the hands of master masons who were trained to reproduce in three dimensions anything an artist drew in two. If skillful engineering was required, it was expected that proper design for it would be contained in the pictures that the masons were given to follow. The ability to draw was the essential skill, and Giotto surely had that.[9] His bell tower is lean and graceful. At a height of 280 feet, it was built as an exception to the city zoning ordinance limiting towers, which is, I think, still in effect today.

There are lots of stories of how Brunelleschi landed the job of designing the cupola while he was still in his twenties. According to Vasari, he had recently come in second in the competition to do the famous doors of the baptistery.[10] He went off to Rome with his young friend Donatello to solace his disappointment by looking at the remains of the Roman capitol.

They could hardly have seen any substantial Roman ruin before and the effect was startling. Donatello's creative urge burst forth in a host of figures, crucifixes, mounted warriors like the Gatamalata of Padua, and heartbreaking representations such as the old Magdalena, mourning her Lord in the desert, a wooden statue in which her nakedness is covered only by the lengthy remains of her once-

---

[9] This is a notion that Frank Lloyd Wright also espoused in more recent years. I don't know if Gustav Eiffel was trained as a *Beaux Artes* painter, but it wouldn't surprise me if he were. And, of course, Samuel Morse earned his living as a very good portrait painter long before he took up electrical engineering and invented the telegraph, proving that good draftsmanship can lead to almost anything.

[10] Vasari's *Lives of the Most Excellent Painters, Sculptors and Architects* is the original and best history of art. Unfortunately it is also one of the least accurate. In any case, Ghiberti won the competition and spent the greater part of the rest of his life in modeling and casting these gilded bronze doors, as well as the later set that were later termed "the gates of paradise." Some historians say that Donatello was too young to have been in on the original competition.

luxurious hair. He also sculpted the first male nude since Greek and Roman times, a little garden statue of the naked boy David, wearing a fancy helmet and holding an enormous sword with which he has removed Goliath's head. It quietly stands today in the second floor of the Museo Bargello.

But Brunelleschi had a different reaction to the Roman visit. He gave up sculpture altogether and concentrated his mind and immense talent on architecture. All the great artists of the Renaissance seemed to be able to go from one of the visual or plastic arts to another, and many practiced art and architecture at the same time. Michelangelo complained that Pope Julius II wanted him to paint when he was really a sculptor. He was obviously both, as well as an architect. Leonardo was similarly polymathic.

But this first experience with the ancient classical temples and the Colosseum turned the youthful Filippo toward the design of neoclassical structures, and he did nothing else for the rest of his life. He measured and drew the remains of the Roman buildings and gathered the inspiration for a true rebirth of Roman architecture.[11]

When he returned to Florence he still had little or no practical experience in architecture or engineering, but he volunteered to solve the problem of vaulting the cupola of the cathedral. He also refused to present a scale model of his plans to the jury in charge of selecting

---

[11] There was much more of the great Roman arena to be seen in Brunelleschi's time than we can visit now. The circuit of the oval and most of the seating was still intact until Pope Julius II got work under way on the Basilica of St. Peter. The architect, Bramante, and his masons used the huge amphitheater as a quarry. Destruction of Roman antiquities was eventually halted by Alexander VI (Lucrezia Borgia's father), but much of the damage had already been done. Most of the immense Flavian Amphitheater is in pieces, inside the Basilica of St. Peter, perhaps a fitting eventuation for a wonderful piece of architecture dedicated to cruelty, torture, and persecution.

the designer and *capomaestro* of the great dome. He is said to have pointed out that anyone could solve the problems once he had shown them how. To convince them of this, he demonstrated how to make an egg stand on end (by bashing in one end on the table) after the assembled elders had said it was impossible. He was eventually given the commission with the proviso that he accept the supervision of an older architect, Lorenzo Ghiberti, who had nosed him out on the competition to create the doors of the baptistery. Filippo agreed, and then called in sick on the first day of work at the site of the cathedral. He sent word that the older man would show the workmen where and how they should begin. The distinguished architect had no idea of how to proceed, and after pondering the problem for a while, left the job to Brunelleschi alone. [12]

If you visit the Museum of the duomo you can see many of the inventions he used to create the double-shelled Gothic dome, its base standing on a great masonry drum that rises above the nave of the cathedral. The lower tiers of stone are wrapped in great iron-bound "chains" of hard sandstone held together with embedded lead-clad iron fastenings that check the thrust of hundreds of tons of limestone pressing down and outward from above. Filippo designed interlocking bricks that were laid in rings so that each tier would support itself as the structure rose. In the space between the shells he constructed kitchens to feed the masons their lunch so that time would not be lost by following the 300-foot climb up and down more than once a day. He carved the keystones and interlocking blocks of limestone by showing the necessary details to the masons, carving them from a turnip or a block of wood. Today you can follow the dizzying climb of the artisans and the designer

---

[12] For more information, read *Brunelleschi's Dome* by Ross King.

and emerge in the enormous lantern, as big as a chapel in its own right, at the breathtaking summit of the cupola.[13]

Our lodging with the young philosophy student was on the Por San Maria, which is the street that connects the Ponte Vecchio with the Piazza della Signoria. This piazza is to my mind one of the three best public spaces in Italy.[14] Entering from the famous bridge from the south or from the railroad station on the west side, you are immediately confronted by the rugged simplicity of the Palazzo Vecchio, its slender tower rising off-center from the great block of the old seat of government. Arnolfo di Cambio also designed this severe building in the late fourteenth century. I decided to climb as much as was possible and managed to get up to the parapet above the upper palace rooms where the early rulers of the commune gloried in their wealth and power before the real authority devolved upon the Medici family, private citizens whose great success as

---

[13] The size of the Cathedral of Florence is hard to grasp in contrast with what had come before. The tallest of the Gothic cathedrals of France was that of Beauvais, which topped out at 157 feet and spanned 51 feet. In spite of many flying buttresses, it fell a dozen years after it was completed, shortly before Arnolfo da Cambio began work on Santa Maria del Fiore. The job left to Filippo called for a vault that *began* at the edge of the drum, *170 feet above the street level!* From there the dome was to vault 143 feet across the void, 92 feet 6 inches more than the breadth of the vaulting of the slender French cathedral. The dome is over 300 feet tall and the lantern on the top reaches close to 400 feet. It was the largest church in the world when built and still only second to Saint Peter's in Rome and St. John the Divine in New York, which is longer but not as high. The span of Brunelleschi's dome was not exceeded until the Superdome was built in New Orleans in the last century.

[14] The other two are the Piazza Navona in downtown Rome and the Piazza San Marco in Venice. The three are very different. San Marco has dignity and bespeaks wealth. The Navona is for the beautiful people, gelato, street artists, and late-afternoon *aperitivi*. The Piazza della Signoria allows us to be surrounded by works of art and architecture. The place is filled with people who come to look at them. But every visitor should have the right to choose his or her own best spaces in Italy. You may prefer the beautiful sloping shell of the Campo of Siena, the glass-domed Galleria Vittorio Emanuele in the center of Milan, or the busy and cheerful Campo de' Fiori in Rome. Italy is studded with wonderful public spaces, laid out hundreds of years ago, and carefully tended and protected by sensitive authority through the centuries.

bankers gave them the mantle of leadership. The political strength of the Medici came from their support of progressive taxation that relieved the burdens of the poor.

They built their "offices," the Uffizi, next door, and it was from there that the real government of the city came to be centered in the sixteenth century. Although I never got to the final stages of the 300-foot crest of the tall slim tower of the Palazzo Vecchio, I did climb high enough to look down on the square and patterned paving stones. There is a clear marker showing the very spot where the firebrand monk, Girolamo Savonarola, was hanged and burnt in 1498. This was the square where old Cosimo de Medici had walked the streets almost unattended sixty years before and negotiated his banking business in the open air.

To my right I could see the huge bulk of the cathedral, its green and white marble casing newly cleaned and splendid to behold. Brunelleschi's dome with its rosy tiles totally dominates the skyline, even though Giotto's elegant and slender campanile and the towers of the Badia, the Bargello, and a half-dozen other great churches punch upward through the mass of golden stucco and terra-cotta tile all around. Down below, the Loggia di Lanzi presents its wonderful gallery of mannerist sculptures to the tourists in the square. It really is quite remarkable that among the churches of Florence, this square presents not only Michelangelo's ideal of male nakedness, but also Giambologna's amazing statue of the Rape of the Sabine Women, showing a plump young woman without clothes being carried high in the air by an undraped youth who fends off her equally naked father with his leg. Somehow I can't see the town fathers of any American capital approving such a civic monument, although millions come here to admire the skill and taste with which these representations of the ancient myths are presented.

I did not tarry long on top of the terraces of the Palazzo Vecchio. There was more to be seen in the state rooms on the way down where Vasari redecorated the century-old apartments to the level of grandeur suitable for the government of the city that lead the artistic world. Back down in the piazza, I walked away from the old center of Florentine government to the marble plaque in the stony street that marked the spot where the fire was kindled to consume the bodies of Savonarola and his two anonymous companion monks.

Although his harsh puritanism is not at all to our taste today, it is hard not to admire the tough spiritual leader. He re-created a republican form of government in Florence in the same age that Columbus was employed by racist and bigoted absolute rulers of Spain. It was also a time when the monumental corruption of the papacy left the church in the hands of Pope Alexander VI Borgia who was enjoying dancing girls at his dinner parties in the Vatican and planning still further political marriages for his pretty daughter Lucrezia. Even Alexander himself was somewhat in awe of the Dominican monk and hesitated for a long time before condemning him. At one point he offered Savonarola the red hat of a cardinal if he would only desist from his inflammatory preaching. The monk refused the hat, stayed still for a few months and then burst forth with another condemnation of immorality. He called for yet another bonfire of the vanities. Both Michelangelo and Sandro Botticelli underwent profound spiritual conversions under the influence of his sermons. Finally the efficacious persuasion of torture wrenched enough incriminating evidence from him that after three trials, the civil authorities executed him, hanging in the smoke of his funeral pyre, muttering *Gesu! Gesu!* until he expired and the burnt limbs fell off his body. His ashes were cast into the all-receiving waters of the Arno to prevent their collection as the relics of a martyr. Neither in his own century nor since has he ever been considered a heretic; merely a troublemaker.

This center of the city is, of course, the place where Michelangelo secured his popularity and reputation by turning a huge flawed block of pure white marble into the most famous male nude in the history of art, his statue of David. This is not a representation of the little boy with a slingshot, but a fully mature young man with the sling on his shoulder, looking accusingly from under his tumbled locks. There is no sign of his Philistine adversary anywhere about. A very good copy stands today where the original reposed for three centuries at the entry to the Palazzo Vecchio until the city fathers decided to rescue it from the pollution of the industrial revolution and had it moved indoors to the Galleria dell'Accademia. The copy is fine in its place, surrounded by teenagers eating *gelato* as usual. The real statue can be seen in the Accademia where it has a shrine that makes it seem even larger than the copy in the piazza. Today almost no one seems startled by this powerful statue's almost casual display of male genitalia, even underscoring Michelangelo's neglect of the incontrovertible fact that the historical David, a traditional Jew, was surely circumcised and the statue is not.

To my right, as I looked at the reproduction David standing in the chilly noon sunshine, are the severe colonnades of the Uffizi, the "Offices" of the Medici bankers who became the rulers of Florence in the fifteenth and sixteenth centuries. Along with the Bargello, the Accademia, and the Palazzo Vecchio itself, these buildings contain the greatest collections of painting and sculpture in the world. There are, by the way, ways of getting reservations for admission to the Uffizi. They seem to be available on the Internet, by telephone, and (it is said) at the Santa Maria Novella Railroad Station. Without a reservation, the lines at the doors of this most famous of all Italian art collections are always long.

In recent years, museum visiting has become even more popular than it was earlier in this century. I speculate that the reason for the congestion may be the maturing of the post–World War II generation of Americans into the golden years and a desire to cash in on the experience with History of Art 101. Most of the visitors are European, however, and many are young. The whole society is better educated and more eager to experience the works of art of their own heritage. But however long the lines, the visitor must go if only to experience Botticelli's aforementioned huge allegorical paintings, *Spring* and *The Birth of Venus*. There are also works by European painters of a half-dozen centuries from as many countries beyond Italy: Albrecht Dürer, Lucas Cranach, Hans Memling (whose virgins, despite bearing a faint resemblance to Popeye's girlfriend Olive Oyl, are exquisitely painted and teeming with natural details from the increasingly prosperous quality of life in Renaissance Germany), and Hans Holbein's brilliant portrait of Sir Richard Southwell. Many were new to us when we first toured the Uffizi, Michelangelo's circular Holy Family which displays Jesus, Mary, and Joseph out in the countryside where they are surrounded by a veritable nudist colony of young men and boys. Titian (or Tiziano, as he is known at home) is represented by the luxurious flesh of the Venus of Urbino, whose attendant servants are searching a wardrobe chest as though looking for something to cover up the reclining beauty. Dosso Dossi, Tintoretto, Paulo Veronese, Peter Paul Rubens, and, of course, Rembrandt Van Rijn are all here. Finally, there are a couple of Canaletto's precise and still dreamy cityscapes of Venice which I would choose if I could have something from the Uffizi to carry home.

Even harder to get into is the Corridoio di Vasari, the private passageway that allowed the later Medici to pass from the Pitti Palace to the Uffizi without exposing themselves to the dangers of the street. They used its half-mile of wall space to hang the portraits of the artists of the centuries. Many of them are self-portraits: Raphael, Bernini, Velazquez, Rembrandt, Joshua Reynolds, Jean Dominique Ingres, Corot, Delacroix, Jacques-Louis David, and the rare and lovely lady painters, Angelica Kauffmann and Elizabeth Vigée-Lebrun. It is possible to make arrangements to visit the Corridor, but we have not been able to do so as yet. Being not among the rich, we could not take this preferred river crossing of the Medici; instead, we strolled over the Ponte Vecchio. If you turn right as you come off the ancient bridge and work your way along Borgo San Jacopo, eventually you will get by several jogs to Santa Maria del Carmine, where you will find Masaccio and Masolino's frescos of the Garden of Eden and the Expulsion from Paradise. Along the way you will have passed the much larger church of Santo Spirito, where the cool lavender-gray columns and pale-yellow buff walls and vaults stand in sharp contrast to the more ornate interiors in Florence. This one is by Filippo Brunelleschi, and the classical detail and cleanliness of line show how pleasantly he introduced the Renaissance of Roman architecture to his hometown in the early *quattrocento*.

But this first look at Oltrarno is just an antipasto to the real event. Motor-buzzed and tourist-thronged it may be, but remember, Firenze itself was the birthplace of the greatest works of art and architecture of the last millennium. How this small city could come to contain so much is a wonder now as it must have been more than seven centuries ago when it was growing from a center of cloth manufacture and finance and putting forth the great burst of creativity that defined the Renaissance. Before our most recent trip we had visited it several times, but despaired of describing it with any degree of justice or even usefulness. After our fourth trip I resolved to make a fist of getting the town into a brief, manageable description. Knowing that such condensation would surely result in failure, we pressed on, regardless, and gave it a try. There is just so much here that it really does overload the senses.

One of the stops along the way as you cross the river is underneath a discreet little balcony that looks down into the Church of Santa Felicità, where the busy grand dukes of Tuscany, transiting their private corridor, could pause to say their prayers or attend Mass in secluded privacy. The gem of that small church, however, is the tiny Capponi Chapel under the feet of the presiding royalty, and thus invisible to them. Here we came with no line to wait in and only a handful of others joining us. Bronzino frescoed one wall with his small, brilliant conception of the Annunciation (1528), the Virgin a lovely peasant girl with a simple shawl and veil. Mary is startled, submissive, curious, and as lovely as the dawn in that moment when she hears the news of her maternity from the Angel. Gabriel is a powerful being floating across the way, but unable to gaze directly on such astonishing perfection as his spiritual vision could discern, he averts his eyes as though struck blind by the sight of the sinless maiden. This fresco is cleaned and remounted on its original wall with what a guidebook called "the clumsy restorations of the eighteenth and nineteenth centuries" removed.[15]

---

[15] Restoration of works of art is a major industry in Italy. They have gotten better at it over the years, and now they leave great gaps in damaged frescoes rather than trying to repaint them to look as they originally did. One of the rules is that whatever is added now must be removable when techniques may have improved later on. The restorer's trade is an old one, and has given current usage to a common word in our language. Missing pieces of marble statuary from Roman times were patched with sealing wax, tinted so cleverly to match the stone that it took an eagle eye to notice it. Perfect pieces of marble were labeled in Latin as *sin cerà*, "without wax," from which we get our word *sincere*.

On the other wall Pontormo created a heart-rending deposition of the battered and lifeless but still perfect body of Christ, supported by angelic helpers and beautiful young women who assist a tragically bereaved Mary. The colors are pale pink, buff, green, and light blue. Everything gleams with the hue of glory except the brown cloak of a single figure lost in contemplation at the edge of the scene, a self-portrait of Pontormo himself.

Santa Felicita is across the ancient bridge into the quarter known as Oltrarno "beyond the Arno." Crossing the Ponte Vecchio to visit it takes you through one of the sights of the town, the bridge flanked with the shops of jewelers and goldsmiths now as it has been since the butchers were banished to other quarters before 1400. Here tourists buy gold, which is sold by weight, measured in small balance scales, and can count on an honest price enforced now as it was in the time of the Medici.

Oltrarno has some fine restaurants with modest prices. We enjoyed Le Volpe e Luna, which was someplace up the first left beyond the bridge. There were others farther down the Borgo San Jacopo to the right. At the time of our last visit there was a wonderful Internet café on the Borgo not sixty meters beyond the bridge. This facility had about forty terminals and an obliging management. The riverside end of the long, narrow store was one large window looking out over the Arno where Cathy was pleased to enjoy the view while I pounded out e-mails to children and collected our own incoming traffic.

Farther down east is the Chiesa di Santo Spirito where Brunelleschi's classical design resulted in a severe nave with great gray columns supporting Roman arches that sprout from Corinthian capitals. The stucco work of the walls is creamy and the architectural elements seem almost blue; all was planned to be restrained and cool.

Of course it could not stay that way for six hundred years. In a few centuries the altar and sanctuary were redone by Giovanni Caccini, who produced a baldichino (perhaps it is a ciborium) of multicolored marble intarsia with dark green-veined marble columns holding up the highly ornamented structure above. Poor Filippo would have regretted the noisy elaboration of his simple structure, but what can you do? People with money will decorate almost anything.

Back in Florence proper, we made an excursion to the east of the Piazza della Signoria, and approached the Bargello, the oldest surviving seat of government in Florence. It was started in the thirteenth century, probably by the teacher and master of Arnolfo di Cambio who later went on to design the Palazzo dei Priori, which replaced its governmental purpose and became known as the Palazzo Vecchio. The Bargello was reduced to being the central police station and seems to have taken its name from a Florentine dialect word for the headquarters of the cops. By the 1860s, when Italy was unified under the constitutional monarchy of Victor Immanuel, it became the first National Museum, a title it still retains.

We started up the wonderful stair toward the great gallery, but were stopped by the sight of a landing curtained in transparent plastic where white-coated conservators were working on a brightly colored equestrian statue, rubbing little bits of it very carefully with Q-tips dipped in tiny bottles of mysterious solutions. The horse and its charming rider turned out to be an early wooden sculpture by Jacopo della Quercia. We had only been familiar with della Quercia from his marvelous marble high reliefs of the creation of man around the central portal of the Basilica of San Petronius in Bologna. But here in wood, polychrome, and gilding, he had produced a fresh and wonderful likeness of St. Martin in the act of giving his cloak to the homeless and impoverished man of Tours. The work had only been discovered a few years before and by now has been put in a proper place in the Bargello. It should perhaps grace a church where it would display the fact that God and His Saints want us to care for the urban poor.

Donatello's San Georgio is also one of the great features of this museum. It originally occupied a niche on Orsanmichele but was removed to the Bargello to protect it from the acid atmosphere of the era of the internal combustion engine. We paid it due reverence as we did the trial pieces submitted for the famous "doors" competition by Ghiberti and Brunelleschi. Donatello's little David, naked with his outrageous hat and boots, is also here. Much of this collection came from the overcrowding of the Uffizi when the last Medici princess willed the entire centuries-old collection to the people of Florence and the new Italian nation in the mid-nineteenth century.

Donatello's Nude David in the Bargello

On toward the east end of the town is Santa Croce, which stands in elevated Gothic grace behind the clean lines of another of Arnolfo di Cambio's elegant fourteenth-century facades. It doesn't quite dominate its piazza, which some critics have said is too big for the church. Inside are the monuments commemorating the tombs of many of the famous Florentine families of the earlier centuries. Started in 1296, the church—which the Franciscans wished to be a place of prayer rather than family glorification—has become a sort of pantheon of the great Florentines. Michelangelo is buried here and, somewhat

Donatello's garden statue of David was the first nude presented to public view for more than a thousand years.

more surprisingly, so is Galileo Galilei, whose intellectual overthrow of the orthodox, fundamentalist teachings of the church almost merited him a fiery end like that of Giordano Bruno. Being a Copernican in cosmology was often dangerous to one's health, even as late as the seventeenth century.

But we found still more wonderful works of art in this "east end" of the city, in the Convent of San Marco. Here the Dominicans gathered to live their conventual life in a wonderful building given by Cosimo Il Vecchio in the early middle of the fifteenth century. Michelozzo designed the cloister and the forty or fifty cells for the monks, including one for Cosimo himself, who came there to pray and recover his composure from time to time. Each cell is decorated with a picture designed to promote meditation. The artist was Fra Angelico and the series of lovely Madonnas with attendant angels are gentle but spectacularly beautiful. The last cell at the end of the corridor on the upper floor was reserved for the prior and thus was home to Savonarola during the years when he preached his condemnation of the "vanities" to the hypnotized Florentines in the tumultuous time when Columbus was out on the high seas discovering a new world.

But the convent of San Marco came into disfavor with the people a number of years later, probably because of the connection between the various orders of monks and the unpopularity of the Inquisition or the rising anticlericalism of the later centuries. The convent was taken from the Franciscans and made into a museum, appropriately set up to house all of the works of Fra Angelico. Here you will find his great Annunciations[16] and a Crucifixion that it is

---

[16] Cathy's all-time favorite Annunciation is the Fra Angelico in Cortona. Mine is the wonderful pair of figures by Pontormo in the tiny chapel in Santa Felicita, across the river in Oltrarno. Exploring Italy in search of "the best" Annunciations is a wonderful hobby and one that will not be soon exhausted.

said he painted while weeping at the moving sight of his own creation. Angelico was so devout and made painting such an act of worship that there is talk of declaring him a saint even today. He is thus in total contrast to Fra Lippo Lippi, who managed to have sex with the young nun acting as his model of holiness and purity. The two artist friars did some of the most beautiful of all renderings of the Virgin. Their religious practice could not have been more different.

Just off the northeast corner of the Piazza Santa Croce we found a family-run trattoria, La Maremma, which had been recommended to us by friends as being both an excellent table and a bargain place to eat. It was also mentioned in two guidebooks, a multiplicity of notice that made me worry that it might have become a tourist trap. Far from it. We had a splendid dinner. In spite of a clientele of Germans, Americans, and Japanese, the polyglot waiter maintained a dignified and efficient pace through a simple supper of a thick and steamy *ribbolita* followed by grilled salmon and a large shareable salad. Their *vino bianco della casa,* as always seems to be the case in Italy, was as good or perhaps better than anything we pour from a newly broached bottle at home.

On another day we set forth up the Lungarno to the West to find the Chiesa di Ognissanti. We had made two other journeys in search of the Ghirlandaio *Last Supper* in the cloister. It was rumored to be open in the early mornings of Monday, Tuesday, and Saturday, but closed by noon. The time and the rarity of its availability made us hurry along the verge of the river and the weather was chilly, a bit windy and punctuated with a few sprinkles. The church was of interest, being decorated in what the American Express Guide called the "best boudoir seventeenth-century baroque style," but we could discern no *Ultima Cena* among its paintings. Then we discovered a discreet card directing us to the cloister next door. The arcades around the little open courtyard sheltered a series of saints done by seventeenth-century artists of what the British call "the second eleven."

We wandered about looking for Ghirlandaio and found nothing, until a knowledgeable Italian wearing his black raincoat like a cape showed up and began to knock loudly at a door at the far side of the courtyard. There was also a bell to ring. Nothing seemed to come of this, but rather suddenly a small, partially disabled woman came in from the street and took up our cause. She shouted in through the door communicator for her husband, the janitor. Then she retreated to the street again. In about ten minutes the little group of twenty which had started on the pilgrimage was reduced to eight, but our faith and persistence were rewarded. A man with a long and ancient key arrived to unlock the door of the old refectory. It was worth the wait.

Ghirlandaio had a wonderful sense of physical reality (as exemplified by the old man he painted elsewhere, posing with a young boy whose beauty is accentuated by the rather dreadful growth on the old man's nose). Here across a twenty-five-foot wall at the end of the friars' dining room, he crowds the twelve and their Master in a space almost bisected by the corbel of the arch holding up the vaulting of the refectory wall. That the cenacle is an upper room is clear from the lemon and orange trees whose tops appear beyond the arched openings, above the heads of the apostles. Judas alone sits in front of the table, his back to us and his face in profile. He looks cocky and self-assured clutching his little leather bag of silver pieces. Peter is scowling at him, fingering what looks like a large bread knife, perhaps a prefigurement of the swipe he takes at the ear of the high priest's servant later in the evening.

For 1480 the whole composition looks quite modern. The small details of table and linen are marvelous. Ruskin thought this was the top of the line when he wrote about the art of Florence in the nineteenth century.

But bests and betters are hard to assign in Florence. Where, for example, could you rank Paolo Uccello's various versions of *The Battle of San Romano.* The one in the Uffizi has rearing, kicking, and frisking horses in orange, salmon pink, white, and black. The forest of raised lances are yellow and red. The armored soldiers and knights are gray and black. The riot of unmodulated color adds to the chaos of battle and, to my eyes, was reminiscent of the monochromatic coloring of many of the *Fauves* or the American nonobjective painters of the 1950s and '60s. All three versions of Uccello's battle scene were done around 1456. The one in Florence is a particularly extravagant riot of contrasting color and light, surely one of the great works of the *quattrocento.* The other two are in Paris and London. Which one is best? Does it matter?

Right across the river from Ognissanti is the Church of the Carmine where one of the great chapels is situated pleasantly removed from the busiest tourist destinations of downtown Florence. The Brancacci family commissioned Masolino to fresco the exquisite little space in 1420, but he was soon joined by the young Masaccio. Their versions of Adam and Eve on opposite walls are amazing. Masolino's ancestral pair are peacefully naked and a little stiff in their pose. Masaccio's discovered sinners retreating from the angel with expressions of horror and loss, every line of their beautiful bodies bespeaking their knowledge of the difference between good and evil and the reality of the terrible deed they have done. This naked pair is a long distance from the medieval representations of the fall of man.

But the rest of the Brancacci chapel is perhaps even more famous, presenting as it does a realistic city background of fifteenth-century Florence as a background for a large and stocky Peter who is walking past a naked, emaciated, and obviously ill man kneeling in the street. As the shadow of the apostle falls upon him he seems to rise up with hope, cured by the remote presence of the first prince of the early church.

Masolino and Masaccio did not quite finish the Brancacci chapel. That was done toward the end of the *quattrocento* by Filipino Lippi, who had the skill and humble grace to paint in the style of his predecessors rather than in his own up-to-date fashion. Perhaps we should expect Filipino to have been polite to his elders; a lot of them were kind to him. He was the illegitimate child of Fra Lippo Lippi, the monk with the large libido and his model for his most famous painting of the Virgin. The embarrassing arrival of young Lippi was smoothed over at the behest of Cosimo de Medici, who liked the painting of the very young mother so much that he talked the pope into absolving the two hot-blooded young people from their monastic vows and, it is said, marrying them. The resulting Filipino grew up in the studio of his father and went on to become a great painter in his own right.

The care and rearing of love children in Florence was one of the more admirable social patterns of the late Middle Ages and the Renaissance years. All of Italy presents a considerable contrast to the way in which the English and French, at least in London and Paris, were used to throwing away these unwanted little citizens in poorhouses of the sort described centuries later by Charles Dickens, or turning them loose on the streets to swell the population of cutpurses and prostitutes that were described by John Gay in *The Beggars Opera*. At least in

Florence, where convents still flourished past the years in which they were largely suppressed in England, there were congregations of nuns who maintained foundling hospitals where the unmarried mother could bring her baby and surrender it over to the sisters, who would bring it up and find either a livelihood or a dowry for the child.

One of these shelters was the Ospedale degli Innocenti on the Piazza Santissima Annunziata. The care of foundlings had for more than a century been a special charity of the Silk Guild when they bought the property and commissioned Brunelleschi to design the refuge. His success with the design of the whole building is delicate and wonderful, but most especially fine is the loggia facing the piazza. The arches are accented with circular apertures in the spandrels between them. Brunelleschi wished to leave these circles open, rather like the great circular holes in clerestory of the duomo. But, thankfully, his usually perfect restraint was here violated by the ornamentation of a series of glazed terra-cotta plaques in heavenly blue and white by Andrea della Robbia. These present charming figures of babies in swaddling clothes, some of them kicking the bandages away with their vigorous tiny feet. At the far left-hand side of the arcade is a grill that led to a horizontal wheel where the unobserved mother could leave her infant and ring a bell which would alert the nun inside to rotate the child into the caring environment of the convent.

The Ospedale, built in the early 1420s, is surely one of the earliest Renaissance buildings of all and one of the most charming. We were not able to visit the interior of the building on the morning we were there, for the venerable shelter of the innocents built by the charity of the silk workers so long ago still functions as an orphanage today. I would love to get inside someday; it is said to be decorated with works by Botticelli and Ghirlandaio.

Madonna Allatante

The problem with Florence is that when you are not being stunned by the paintings, you are blasted away by the architecture. Strangely enough, we have not found a similar flowering of music here. We probably were searching at the wrong season, but unlike Milan, Venice, Parma, and Bologna, we have never found a concert or even a church choir performing for our benefit here. I am sure they are about the town somewhere in proper season, but the visual and plastic arts seem more characteristic of this city.

On another visit we crossed the river to the Piazzale Michelangelo and inspected the oldest church in Florence, San Miniato, up on top of the hill overlooking the Piazzale. The bus ride, once discovered, was swift and cheap. The view gives on the Boboli Gardens and the eastern side of the Pitti Palace, the Arno with its bridges, and the great dome of the cathedral flanked by Giotto's bell tower and the spire of the old abbey, The Badia. When the light is right, as it frequently is, it is a gorgeous scene.

Back in town, Orsanmichele is one of the frequently overlooked gems of the center of Florence. We had walked past it a dozen times before we really focused on the grime-encrusted building with its oversized statues standing in dark Gothic niches. Here it was *due passi* (just two steps) from the Hotel Porta Rossa. The niches around the outside of the simple building originally contained some of the great early sculptures of the Renaissance, although others have been removed to the Museo del Opera del Duomo. Verrocchio's *Christ and Doubting Thomas* is here, sheltered by a classical frame and pediment done by Donatello. Around the corner are Ghiberti's John the Baptist and St. Matthew, statues he did in the midst of his interminable commission to create the doors of the baptistery.

Then, one day, we finally ventured inside Orsanmichele to get out of a shower of rain and found (in a state of partial repair) the glowing jewel of Orcagna's tabernacle, which dates all the way back to 1359. Both the tabernacle and the building which it houses are the apex of the lacy, ornamented Gothic style. It is amazing to me how elegantly it sits in comfortable companionship with work of the first of the Renaissance masters. It was commissioned by the wealth of both some victims and some survivors of the great plague, the Black Death. The church itself is, of course, even older, but it was not originally designed to be a church at all. It was dedicated to the Florentine worship of commerce and was at first a grain market surmounted by an elegant warehouse.

At the Vin Santo, a small ristorante just *due passi* south of the Porta Rossa, we had a simple supper of tortellini in brodo, a bit of *baccala*, and an *insalata mista*, all the while wondering why the simple place was named for "holy wine," presumably the kind used at the altar during mass. As we were refusing dessert, I asked the *proprietario* how his place came by its name. I guess I didn't think people drank altar wine, although in my youth, as an altar boy, I confess to having sneaked a taste in the vestry while the priest was out of range. The master of the house smiled and disappeared to reemerge with an ancient bottle and a plate of *cantucci*, the nearly rock-hard oblong biscuits that we had misnamed "biscotti" (if they have sliced almonds in them, they are *cantucci*). But whatever you term them, dipped in the sweet wine made from the last shriveled grapes that had concentrated their sugar clinging to the vine well into the late autumn, they were just fine. Investing in our future taste for his delicacies, the proprietor did not include them on the modest bill.

Every time we have left Florence it has been with a feeling that we have still only begun to know the treasures of the queen city of Tuscany. We must come back to the valley of the Arno many more times.

XVII

CARS AND THEIR PILOTS
The Song of the Open Road

The Italians have always made the most beautiful and fastest cars in the world. The Bugatti of the late 1930s was a legendary vehicle, streamlined more elegantly than any other of its era. The Ferrari and the Maserati are surely among the most expensive and beguiling toys available to the richest, most discriminating drivers today. But Italians don't exactly drive a car. Their word is *guidare*, which is something both more and less than our *drive*. The verb suggests that the magnificent machine, from the tiniest Fiat to the Lancia and Lamborghini, is having its own way with the road, scorching the pavement to its own pleasure. The happy owner behind the wheel is giving it guidance, perhaps urging it on to ever greater feats of power, speed, and traction. But the intention, the will, and the desire are in the body and soul of *la macchina*.

It is said by some statisticians that while the Italians have the greatest number of recorded accidents per hundred thousand kilometers driven in Europe, they have a much lower number of fatalities than most other countries.[1] This may have something to do with the way in

---

[1] The Portuguese are charming, but reputed to be the deadliest drivers.

which statistics are compiled. The Germans and Swedes are ashamed of their accidents, but the Italians flaunt their record of bent fenders and crumpled bumpers as a badge of honor.

And they maintain their cars in gleaming perfection if they are anywhere near new. They treat them with almost reverential respect as honored guests of the family. It is as though the Italian, when taking a surrogate mistress in the form of a 172-CV Turbo, prefers to treat her with the dignity and respect one should accord

1939 Bugatti, 3.3-liter coupe

to a countess, or at least a lady of noble lineage. Washed, waxed, polished, and gleaming in brilliant red or glossy black, she is something between a duchess and a strumpet, and her *fidanzato* is head over heels in love with her.

Unlike the Autobahn of Germany, there are more or less binding speed limits on the great *autostrade* that connect the major cities of the peninsula. The roads are wonderfully engineered, and have reduced traveling time between north and south from days to hours. They are safe, swift, and pleasant driving, even if they stay away from the picturesque and populated towns along the way. But most of us are not ready, at least initially, to maintain a pace that will keep us out of the way of a happy Italian driver, inevitably male and probably a descendant of one of those halberdiers that Pontormo painted. He approaches from the rear at 125 kph while we are lazing along at what seems a breathtaking clip in the left-hand lane of the superhighway. His high-beam headlights start to flash on and off in the noonday light as he approaches. He will not sound his horn until well upon you, so keep an eye out for those flashing lights. These signals, which would be taken as a sign of some hostility in the U.S., are nothing of the sort here. He knew that we would want to move over before he arrived on our rear bumper and he was merely giving a cheery salute, with thanks for not inhibiting his pleasure or forcing him to reduce speed.

This meaning of the flashing lights becomes quite clear on the good secondary roads where there are but two lanes separated by a bright yellow stripe. Stay with the game, keep your speed, but when you see those lights, edge slightly to the right and leave four or five feet available to your companion from the rear. That's all he will need. Flashing brightly to the oncoming traffic, he will straddle the yellow line and pass while the cars in the oncoming lane make a similar shrug of an accommodation to allow him through without ever meeting another vehicle head on.

This is such an expected procedure that I soon got accustomed to it (the two-lane roads are often quite wide), and I knew that sooner or later I would try it myself. From that liberating moment onward, I was no longer the timid patsy that I was when I left the Avis lot at Malpensa Airport. Like Mr. Toad in *The Wind in the Willows*, I too became the Lord of the Open Road, the Terror of the Highway. Off with a cheery wave to those we passed, I found myself happily flashing my headlights at the guy in front, who was dawdling along at 100 kph, just before I dashed on between him and the gleaming diesel Mercedes fourteen-wheeler that was coming the other way down the two-lane strip.

In adopting this local style of guiding a car, however, you should be equipped with something a touch more battle-ready than the Fiat Panda or the Ford Festiva. These little fellows are wonderful cars and much the cheapest to charter, but rapid acceleration is not one of their great virtues. And the ability to go from 80 to 120 kph without a lot of gear changing—when trying to retreat to the right-hand lane if caught short for space—is one of the essentials of the Italian style of pleasure driving.

At least Italians drive from the "proper" side of the car and on the usual U.S. side of the road. This makes it a lot easier to get used to than the classic case of going through an English roundabout and winding up, after making a left turn, full in the teeth of the oncoming traffic. In Italy the cars stay more or less on the side of the road you are expecting them to use. I took up driving in Italy at the age of sixty-four, and found that my eyes and reflexes were perfectly adequate to the demands made upon them. (Now, at eighty, I am a bit more careful.) I even got an "International" driver's license, which is a sort of racket of the automobile clubs: $10 for a permit that has to be renewed *every* year. We were also deceived by the well-kept secret of the VAT (Value Added Tax), which is seldom quoted up front in the rental advertisements. It can be as high as 25 percent now, thus making a considerable difference. Renting in advance from the big U.S. agencies provided a special rate, but the VAT appeared on the credit card statement a month after we got home. Fuel is expensive, but most European cars are real gas misers.

We enjoyed touring by rail and car in turn. The great advantage of the automobile is that it makes the hill towns, country monasteries, and outlying Palladian farmhouses accessible. We discovered a most marvelous lunette of the Virgin and Child by Luca della Robbia over a courtyard doorway in a very obscure monastery along a country road south of Florence. On the same trip we bought a spit-roasted chicken from the itinerant proprietor of a canteen truck in the square of San Gimignano. It provided a fine picnic from the tailgate of the car when we stopped by the side of a canal that tumbled over a small waterfall.

A Fiat Panda stopped for a picnic.

XVIII

SIENA

A Happy Look Backward to the Sorrows of the Middle Ages

We came to Siena from the north by car through southern Tuscany and toured the rolling countryside for several hours. The April landscape was green with silvery olive trees and rich red, newly plowed soil. Each hill was topped with a tuft of woods, a single tree, a stone barn and farmhouse, or, occasionally, an entire village. In one of the villages we stopped at the only *alimentari* and negotiated with a pair of rotund, delightfully friendly ladies for a hero sandwich of noble proportions. It was assembled with great care, replete with *pecorino, pomodoro, prosciutto,* salami, and various assorted vegetables well sprinkled with good olive oil. Sectioned with the Swiss army knife[1] and accompanied by a bottle of local white wine, it might have provided provender for a family for several days had we not dispatched the whole thing in a leisurely picnic along the roadside. I cannot recall the name of the wine, but it came off the shelf of the store, cost about $1.35 in the 1990s, and was just right with that monumental sandwich.

Following the necessary nap in the car, we pressed on to the west and were eventually rewarded by the sight, uphill from us, of the

---

[1] Always have one in your pocket or your shoulder bag when traveling—if the anxious airport security guards in the U.S. don't take it away from you.

wonderful silhouette of Siena's duomo against a pale orange sky. Like most of the cathedrals in Italy, the building is huge. Giovanni Pisano started designing it in the older, Romanesque style. (His father, Nicola Pisano, sculpted the wonderful pulpit.) They worked upward in a layercake of black and white marble bands, building the bicolored columns that look like stacks of checkers, rearing arches and massive buttresses. They eventually finished it with a wonderful dome designed by yet another architect. But before they were done, in the height of the town's prosperity, the powers that were decided to make their cathedral the greatest in the world. This Tower of Babel kind of town planning was generated by an abundance of economic success and overreaching civic pride. Neither the Roman gods nor the Christian deity are very forgiving of this sort of project management. Almost predictably, they lost their next war with Florence, an ongoing Guelph-versus-Ghibelline soccer match that was tied 2–2 at the time. This is what comes of sticking the municipal neck out too far. They had started building the new cathedral by using what is now the nave as crossing and transepts for the enormous structure. The towering arches that were to form the north wall of the great new nave were built, as was most of the west facade. These segments outline what the building was intended to encompass when the great plan was complete. But the setback by Florence turned out to be a relatively permanent condition when the Black Death visited Siena three times in the mid-fourteenth century and almost depopulated the town.[2] The church was finished as we see

---

[2] We have all heard of this plague but most of us know little about it. It may have been bubonic carried by rat fleas, but it might also have been anthrax brought to Europe by shipments of Asian horses. In either case it was swift and deadly. Swellings in the armpits and groin were followed by spitting up blood. Death came in about three days. I don't know how many died in Siena, but the population of Florence dropped from one hundred thousand to less than fifty thousand in the years between 1348 and 1351. Parts of Europe were largely depopulated, and something like 30 percent of the population died in the late fourteenth century. No one knew what caused it or what could stop it, although burning witches, self-flagellation, and the murder of Jews were variously tried as remedies.

it today, and pretty fine at that. Although the gargantuan scale of the project was abandoned, never to be resumed, you can climb a spiral stair inside that freestanding north wall and look out from the parapet on what would have been the line of the eaves above the clerestory. It's an impressive conception.

Siena is colorful in many ways. To begin with, the pigments raw and burnt sienna are made from clays of the local soil whence they are exported around the world. Raw sienna is a nice, gutsy, brownish-yellow; the cooked variety is a rich, ruddy orange-brown that finds a place on virtually every artist's palette. It is also the basic color of all the roof tiles, stucco, and brick in Italy, except in neighboring Umbria where they are, naturally, a little more umber-colored.

But the more exciting accent colors in Siena are the flags of the seventeen *contrade*, the neighborhood divisions of the town that rival each other in the fierce partisanship of their residents. Each neighborhood has a symbol on its banner, delineated in bright primary hues of the full color spectrum. The symbols are an eagle, a snail, a dolphin, a rhinoceros, a turtle, and a porcupine. There are also the owl, the unicorn, a scallop, elephant, caterpillar, dragon, giraffe, goat, panther, wolf, and a duck. Most of the beasts wear crowns, or bear banners in their pictures which adorn the flags you see everywhere. The elephant has a castle on his back and the eagle has two heads. They are a very agreeable menagerie, and I debated buying a set of the flags for some paltry sum at a rather nice tourist stand near the Campo. But what I thought of at the time as better judgment overcame the urge, and having returned home I have ever since regretted my mistaken stinginess. I may someday make a pilgrimage back to Siena just to acquire a set of those wonderful gonfalons. They would look superb as "dressing ship" flags on my little boat on the Connecticut River on the Fourth of July or Labor Day.

The Campo is the scallop-shell-shaped heart of Siena, rimmed by shops and cafés and closed off on the more or less straight northeastern side by the slightly concave facade of the Palazzo Pubblico. On the second floor of this building is the municipal art gallery, which houses wonderful paintings allegorizing good and bad government to the edification of the city council in whose chambers they decorate the walls. It has a bell tower called the Torre del Mangia, a designation which probably has to do with eating but does nothing to detract from its grace and extreme height. The top half-dozen stories of the structure are made of white travertine stone which makes a wonderful contrast with the slim brick shaft. The color scheme reminds me of the white-painted topmasts above the oiled pine spars of the old fishing schooners.[3]

But likening the tower to a mast is hardly appropriate to the scale of the thing; the Torre is 102 meters tall, in the same league with the much earlier Cremona and Modenese spires, and taller than a thirty-story building. Even in this era of steel framing and stressed-skin architecture, a tower of more than 330 feet is impressive. Considering it was made of mortared masonry in a land noted for its earthquakes, it seems almost miraculous that it should be here at all 650 years after it was built as an offering to God for remitting the plagues of the Black Death. Somehow, in spite of its grand scale, it is clearly less an act of hubris than the planned enlargement of the cathedral. We settled into white plastic chairs at a table of an outdoor café on the upper rim of the Campo and watched the tower march through the cloud-flecked blue sky in a nice breeze.

---

[3] There are replicas of the Italian towers in many parts of the world. My favorite is in Waterbury, Connecticut, where a half-scale tower rises gracefully above the railroad station, a symbol of civic pride that matched the attitude of the Sienese of the late Middle Ages. It bespeaks confidence in a prosperous future and the permanence of worldly success, in this case of the New York, New Haven, and Hartford Railroad which went bankrupt in the 1960s.

Our hotel, the Chiusarelli, was a touch down at the heel, but quite clean, comfortable, and at that time less than 100,000 lira for the night. It is located on the busy Viale Curtatone, which runs along a ridge separating the deep lowland that contains Saint Catherine's house from another valley that is the site of the Communal Soccer Stadium. Many Italian towns are built on a series of hills, but Siena seems to have been settled on escarpments, gorges, cliffs, ravines,

Siena Palazzo Publico
1288-1309

and quarry pits in middle-sized mountains. If you plot your course carefully, you can get around town on the ridges without too much climbing. But if you take a straight shot from the great church of St. Dominic to the Campo, you will go down and up the equivalent of five or six stories. Our room at the Chiusarelli looked down on the soccer stadium. Had there been a game, we could have sold seats in our bedroom.

The two midsummer horse races around the Campo for *il Palio* are extolled in all the touristic literature about Siena. They are said to be a great show each time, but they also jam the city with other tourists and take place in the expensive high season. We've not been. Maybe someday.

The art in Siena, both the late medieval Sienese school and the early Renaissance work, is hard to summarize and impossible to catalog here. (For more information about the art of Siena, see my book, *About Italy: Puglia to the Po*.) The cathedral and baptistery together probably contain the best collection, but there is a lot to be seen. This building is replete with works of Pisano, Ghiberti, and Jacopo della Quercia. Upstairs is the duomo proper where the *pavimento* was inlaid with biblical scenes by the best artists, a swatch at a time for over two hundred years, until fifty-six areas were delineated in the floor. Pisano's wonderful pulpit is also here, showing Romulus and Remus being suckled by their adoptive mother, the she-wolf, under the preacher's feet. The building provides enough material for a good course in art history. Thanks offerings to various protecting saints are particularly interesting, whether commemorating being rid of the Nazis in the mid-twentieth century or being spared the wrath of the Florentines in the mid-thirteenth, about equally grisly alternatives to the Sienese of those times. We allowed the greater part of a day for the cathedral, with time out for a good lunch. Even so, we didn't see it all. We resolved to come back again another day to soak in the beauty of this medieval town.

The Renaissance never really got to Siena. The city went straight from the Gothic to a few adventures with the later baroque. The Sienese passed the greatest part of the fifteenth and sixteenth centuries under the scourge of the plague, the heel of Florence, the domination of the Spanish Hapsburg Emperor Charles V, or the elegant iron fist of the Medici. One result has been the preservation of the medieval city, unaltered by Renaissance prosperity, today smiling, sweet, and finally prosperous again.

XIX

ORVIETO
Atop the Stump of an Old Volcano, Surrounded by Grapes

South of Tuscany and Umbria on the way to Rome, we first saw Orvieto as a jagged group of houses and a few towers crowning a massive plug of volcanic rock. The sides of the mountain are impressive cliffs that inspired the Etruscans to make it a stronghold almost three thousand years ago. Even though some of their language can be read today by clever scholars, we still know very little about them. The Romans almost totally obliterated their civilization by making it illegal to speak or write their language. This form of cultural genocide could be remarkably effective in the years before the printing press. Manuscripts were few and inscriptions on monuments terse and uninformative. The Etruscans learned to speak Latin in a generation or so, and their language simply disappeared. Their descendants became Roman in both culture and citizenship. But wherever the hill towns of north-central Italy present their fantastic silhouettes to the sky, you will find evidence that the Etruscans were there first. Huge, roughly shaped stone walls at the very crests of nearly unclimbable heights signal that they settled here eight centuries before the Caesars. I wonder if they had a heroic poetry of their own, full of wars and blood and honor. Or were their forbidding strongholds little courts of safety where love songs were sung and amorous youths and maidens dallied in the warm climate of Latium? That great circular chandelier in Cortona is decorated with figures that surely exalt human desire, whether only of satyrs, bacchantes, or other dancers, I cannot be sure. Will we ever be able to read the Etruscans' songs? Did they sing?

The train stops below the town in the flat valley of the immature Tiber. Buses and taxis scale the crag and eventually deposit tourists in the Piazza del Duomo. Pope Clement VII waited out the horrible sack of Rome here in the early sixteenth century when the various ungoverned mercenary troops of the Emperor Charles V had their savage way with the imperial city. The square in Orvieto is peaceful and hardly seems large enough to support the immense facade of the cathedral that completely dominates the city. It is a stretch to call it a city; composed of less than 25,000 inhabitants on the rock above the plain, the town is less than half the size of Wilmington, North Carolina. I don't know how much smaller it may have been during the early thirteenth century when they raised that lofty pile. It may have been larger then. The changing fortunes of war and plague over the centuries make it hard to say for sure.

On either side of the doors of the cathedral are a series of bas-reliefs that display the same teaching about the creation of man, his *peccato originale*, and the final judgment of the blessed and the damned that was usually depicted on church portals in the Middle Ages and the early Renaissance. The guidebooks are a little vague about who made them and when, but the likely candidate is Lorenzo Maitani, the architect who completed the cathedral and gave the facade its colorful triple gables. He also did much of the interior before his death in 1330. The reliefs are wonderful, delicately modeled, and presage the work of della Quercia in Bologna.

On the left is a most human pair of first parents. A robed God the Father removing Eve from Adam's side with surgical precision, and a pair of vengeful angels hustling the couple out of paradise. Then an oppressed Adam wields a mattock while his still-naked lady looks the other way, sitting like Little Miss Muffet on her tuffet and spinning flax by hand. Almost all of the important scenes of both Old and New Testaments are there, flanking the central portal. On the far right pier there is an orderly tangle of figures showing the resurrection of the dead, their judgment, the ascent of the blessed, and the just desserts coming to those who have failed in this life at the bottom. The panels are separated and connected by twining ivies that seem espaliered on the marble blocks of the pilasters. I have seen nothing like it anywhere else in Europe. These scriptural stories in stone are crowned by huge fantastic bronzes of the emblems of the evangelists: the angel, the lion, the eagle, and the bull. The whole effect is appropriately apocalyptic. For more than six centuries the faithful have been contemplating the beginnings and ends of important things as they pass through those portals. The effect of the whole facade is to put one's own prayer for the petty ups and downs of daily life in a proper perspective.

Inside the cathedral the same themes of death, damnation, resurrection, and salvation are displayed in the frescoes of Luca Signorelli. Begun in the later *quattrocento*, they are often cited as among the earliest of the sort of compositions of crowds of nude figures that became the stock in trade of the mannerist painters in the next century. The Orvieto frescoes of Signorelli are thought to have had a profound influence on the young Michelangelo, who undoubtedly saw and examined them. Today, they have a certain naive quality compared to Michelangelo's work, but they are stunning. While all the medieval and Renaissance artists were quite proficient at conveying the horrors of hell, Signorelli is at the top of the list in showing us the resurrection and the approach to beatitude. His reassembled bodies are coming out of the grave like summer bathers who had been buried for a nap on the beach. They lift themselves from the sands in which they have spent but an afternoon awaiting their release to eternity. They are nearly naked, their loins simply looped with colored scarves of striped Roman silk. Their hair is long, mostly blond, and their bodies are those of late teenagers. Their expressions are wide-eyed with innocent curiosity. While archangelic trumpeters summon them from above with six-foot instruments, other angels play mandolins and guitars to accompany their rising. There is a blithe Woodstock quality to the whole scene.

Perhaps the daily contact with so much great religious art accounts for the virtues of many Italians. The institutional church seems to have little effect on most of them. Their sex lives are untrammeled, their abortions as frequent, and their disrespect for catechetical rules are as flagrant as any people in Europe. Yet they act like St. Francis when they can, and will usually do the Christian thing when their goodwill is called for. Since the preachers don't seem to be the source of such behavior, I think it may come from the art.

While in Orvieto, we sampled their famous wine *in situ*. Ours was a brief stop, and I do feel it would be worthwhile to come back and pass more time here. There are many sights to see and several good hotels and guest houses in town, as well as any number of restaurants. The pace of life seems less heroic here than in the larger cities. I guess that's why the popes used it as a getaway in times of trouble.

XX

ROMA*
The Eternal City

Rome is not like the rest of Italy. There is too much art, too much religion, too great an empire, and more than 260 popes. It is a city not of a people, but of one man: the latest emperor, dictator, or the current successor of the fisherman. And for every statement that might be made about them, there are dozens of exceptions. Even an old *Catholic Encyclopedia Dictionary* suffixes a disclaimer to its assertion that Pius XI was number 261 as "the most reliable number." That would make John Paul, the first Polish pope, number 266 in the line since Peter. But there are also a score or more of antipopes, most of whom reigned in France, and some of them were quite as holy as those who were designated as real popes by the subsequent papacies. The whole collection includes the saintly, the scholarly, the legalistic, the bloody-minded, the ecstatic, the mercenary, the military, the political, the visionary, the punitive, the ignorant, and the wise in generous measure.

Many had huge chunks of the great architecture of the city they took over pulled down to reuse its stone for their own projects. Others have collected and safeguarded the art of past ages and commissioned

---

*We call it Rome, but the Romans call it Roma.

some of the greatest achievements of human imagination. Still others have forbade the teaching of truth for fear it might upset faith. Only a few have taken refuge in the "Doctrine of Infallibility," and those (since Pius IX) really recognized that its proclamation at the first Vatican Council was largely a piece of nineteenth-century theological bravado in the face of the loss of political and military power. Almost all in recent times have been celibate in behavior as well as theory, although Peter was not. But some have had full and abundantly fruitful relationships with women, while others feared women and felt that sexual congress was almost always sinful (even though necessary for the "continuation of the species"). At the very least, modern popes and their doctrinal advisors consider the sexual desire of men and women for each other to be a fundamental source of sin, and among the worst things that can distract mankind from the primacy of another, better world.

Only a few recent popes, such as Pius XII and Paul VI, were intellectuals. John XXIII, whose simplicity of manner masked his commanding intelligence, lived close enough for us to really know him. He was a plain man of great faith who spoke of docility to the promptings of the Holy Spirit and seems to have loved all men, women, children, criminals, sexual deviants, communists, Jews, Muslims, Protestants, peasants, businessmen, babies, and politicians.

Despite its history, there seems to be little in the capital city of the old empire that has much of anything to do with the Carpenter's Son of Nazareth, the Historical Jesus, the Mythic Christ, or the Word of the Gospel of John. Even if you are an American Christian, Catholic, Episcopalian, or denominational Protestant, Rome may or may not reinforce the state of mind you come with. Direct contact with Rome has turned some Catholics into cynical nonbelievers just as it has often confirmed the faith of other pilgrims. The almost magical environments created by Bramante, Michelangelo, Raphael, and Bernini have forced more than a few Anglicans to their knees in a flood of believing tears, not just a response to a sort of theological stage setting, but a recognition of the power of the faith that moved the artists to such titanic achievements. The visible faith of the far-flung church is inspirational; the vast wealth of the papacy is a scandal to many. Rome is not a city to be taken lightly.

Like others over many millennia, we descended into Rome from a higher elevation in the North. The original settlers of Italy must have come through the passes of the Alps either east or west and worked their way south past the chilly lakes of Garda, Iseo, and Maggiore to the sunnier climate of Latium where the Arno and the Tiber intertwine to form a fertile flat land of lumpy hills, somewhat swampy, where a number of tribes coexisted in neighborliness and occasional hostility. The Etruscans were there first, following the original Villa Novans and perhaps the half-mythic Umbrians that the ancients thought were emigrants from Asia Minor.

We descended from an even higher altitude, coming by plane over the tops of the Alps and coasting slowly down beyond the lakes and the Tyrrhenian shore to settle on the smooth tarmac next to the beaches of the fishing village of Fiumicino. This is a very agreeable place to arrive, and the terminal is typically stylish in Italian fashion. We were rapidly passed through a simple customs check of our passports and directed through an elevated corridor past a convenient battery of ATM which gobbled up our dollars for an adequate if not generous ration of euros.

Rome is, of course, like all the great modern cities, not a total unity, but an interlocking series of neighborhoods whose denizens, in many cases, are separated by class, economic status, and, sometimes, political history and loyalty. As we mounted to the express tracks following signs for the Stazione Roma Termine, we passed through several historical eras with their memories of those imprisoned while waiting to be martyrs of the time of Diocletian and other second-century emperors. Leftover self-congratulatory statues (in giant scale) of Constantine, the first Christian emperor, are strewn about the further center of town, mostly in the Forum. This area, rebuilt and redecorated by a number of generations of the strong men and brutes that held power here, is the site of the lowland that the tribes of the fabled seven hills used as a meeting place for public discussion after they had cooperated in the world's first civic drainage project: building the great *cloaca maxima*, which still takes surplus water from the city to the all-embracing and swiftly flowing depths of the Tiber.

Getting from the *termini* to our goal in the southeastern quarter of Rome takes a taxi ride past most of the important civic buildings of the modern town to a triangular projection into the curve of the Tiber, the location of the Campus Martius, a quarter of the old town devoted to military exercise. This is where Pompey, flushed with the success of his looting before Caesar overcame him, strove to cement his popularity by presenting Rome with its first all-weather stone theater. Part of its outline is preserved in the curved shape of street behind the church of St. Andrea della Valle. Our small hotel, called the Albergo di Teatro di Pompeo, is located here, on the Largo del Pallaro, almost at the spot where Julius Caesar was murdered by those who thought he was too ambitious to reestablish the royalty of the ancient kings of the then-republican city. The exterior of the hotel is unimpressive and its lobby small, but its rooms are large, neat, and comfortable. The basement breakfast room is in the remodeled space of the foundation of the original theater, the *colazione* delicious, and the ristorante of the same name in the next block both a gustatory delight and of manageable expense.

In this neighborhood, there are many modest hotels of relatively low tariff, but having stayed at many of them, we have developed an affection for the Teatro di Pompeo and returned to it often. Next to the entry of the hotel there is a gloomy underpass into one of the most charming and useful small piazze in Rome, the Campo de' Fiori, the "Field of Flowers." From early morning until midday, the Campo is the site of Rome's best daily market. Everything is for sale, from elegant footwear to swordfish, from handbags and silk cravats to sexy or plain undergarments, from kitchen equipment to DVDs.

Rome may not have been built in a day, or even in a millennium, but it is actually something of an upstart in the Mediterranean world. It is really a relatively young city in world terms despite the legend of its eternity. The cities of the river valleys of the Nile, the Euphrates, the Indus, and the Yellow rivers are far, far older. Even Carthage was senior to its eventual conqueror, as were the Greek communities of Sicily and the southern part of the boot. Older still were the great classical centers of Athens, Sparta, and Corinth. Delphi was older than anything in Italy, and it came later than Troy, Mycenae, and Thebes. The traditional date of the first construction of a mythical wall at Rome is 753 BC, when Remus challenged his wolf-suckled twin brother by leaping over the other's half-built city wall and precipitating the fight that led to his death. This date is probably pretty close to a true estimation of the time when the local peoples decided to gather themselves into a community. On several of the traditional seven hills there were a number of mutually distrustful tribes who fortified the heights with defensive structures sometime in the eighth century BC. Hill settlements also unwittingly protected their inhabitants from the malaria of the low wetlands near the Tiber. Although no one knew that it mattered at the time, mosquitoes don't fly very high above their natal swamps.

Like all of the great metropolises of the world, Rome today is really a series of neighborhoods, almost small towns or cities in themselves. They are connected by tubes, boulevards, avenues, paths, and alleyways. In New York you can live for years in Greenwich Village and never experience Brooklyn, or even the Upper East Side, or Harlem. Still, you can consider yourself a New Yorker. People who grew up on the South Side of Chicago can be as separated by experience from Evanston as are Neapolitans and Romans who meet by chance in Liguria. There are people living in the EUR, Mussolini's ideal city on the south side of Rome, who have never been to the Spanish Steps. Although closer in actual distance, Trastevere, across the Tiber, is at a great physical and psychological distance from the fashionable Via Veneto. And international travelers taking the train from the airport at Fiumicino see a very different Rome from those who arrive by car via the various Autostrade that feed into the Grande Raccordo Anulare, the great ring road that circles the city.

We have come to Rome both ways and learned something of the different aspects of the city in the process. Suburbs of Rome from the windows of a train are tired, grubby, and somewhat depressing, except for the rare moments when you suddenly catch a glimpse of one of those ranks of serried arches of an aqueduct built eighteen centuries ago. In a rented car we once approached the city with the anxiety of returning the vehicle by the required time after we had dropped off our bags at a hotel. The advantage of its being a Sunday with less traffic was balanced by the fact that the Auto Europe office was scheduled to close at 12:30.

We spent the early morning cruising through a pretty but undistinguished, lumpy green countryside studded with ordinary cinder-brick and stucco houses, some small barns, and a few thin rows of poplars dividing field and fallow. Then suddenly we saw a distant blue shape rising above the horizon of the countryside landscape, a smooth, oval derby-hat shape with studs and a topknot. It was the huge dome of Saint Peter's looming over the edge of a low hill, still nearly ten miles away. Michelangelo's domed center of Christendom seen from far away bulks larger than it does from the middle of the city, much larger than it does from the old downtown of Rome on the other side of the Tiber, and far larger than it appears from the piazza in front of the great building. The proportions of what looks like a two-story facade are so perfect that the building appears much smaller than it actually is. The facade is the work of Gian Lorenzo Bernini, who extended Bramante's original nave to almost double the size of the huge church. The result is that the dome can hardly be seen at all from the Piazza San Pietro within the embrace of the colonnade Bernini also added to the original plan.

The wonderful mythic literature of the earliest times of Rome is recounted in the work of Livy. His history includes the story of the Rape of the Sabines, seemingly more of an insistence on favorable marriages than criminal rape in our sense. Supposedly the Roman men, mostly a warrior band, lacked wives and carried off all the Sabine girls they could find at a festival they had arranged to attract them. The Romans promised to honor their new brides and the girls contrived to adjust to their forcible matrimony. After some passage of time, the fathers and brothers of the assaulted girls mounted an attack on the contentedly wed Romans. In the midst of the battle the young women flung themselves into the fray, their tunics in *negligee* and their hair unbound. They placed themselves between the contestants, telling both to stop trying to kill their husbands, brothers, or fathers, as the case may have been. Livy says that the men on both sides were struck dumb at the sight. They agreed to settle their differences by recognizing their new relationships. Whatever actually happened, the tribes living on the hills were merging into one city population. Self-conscious nationalism was growing out of heroic example. Freeing a unified Rome from a later attempt at Etruscan reconquest is the matter of the legend of Horatius at the Bridge, captured in a poem by Thomas Babington Macaulay, who conveys a wonderful feeling for the nineteenth-century attutide toward ancient Roma.

The community of the small highlands became first a city of brick, and later, according to Augustus, who became the first emperor, it was changed to one of marble—or at least one in which the brick and concrete was encased in marble. It eventually spread over all the hills, but to the east was a lower field, a broad meadow outside the original walls of the first of the Etruscan kings who governed in the sixth century. It was called the Campus Martius, an area described as a greensward that filled the space inside the great loop the Tiber makes toward the Vatican and Janiculum hills. As its name suggests, it was used for military exercises, combat training, and close-order drill. Possibly, for this reason it was one of the last areas built upon in classical times. At the end of the time of the republic, Pompey, an ambitious politician contesting with Julius Caesar for the palm of preferment, built Rome's first stone theater there, a gesture that brought him great credit with the fickle common people, the *mobile vulgus* that we refer to as "the mob."

Pompey was selected as consul while at the head of a considerable army. He was technically too young for the position, but his brilliant generalship carried the day and led to his reputation. He had also become marvelously rich from the loot taken during his conquests in Spain and Asia. Later Caesar and Pompey fought a private war all around the northern side and eastern end of the Mediterranean. Caesar won. Pompey was done in by the Egyptians, who were hoping to curry favor with the victor. Thence followed the plot and assassination of Caesar by self-styled guardians of the Republic, and then the careful political creation of the role of emperor by Octavian, who took the title of Augustus. He maintained all the forms of the Republic but took all real authority for himself. His skillful machinations led to almost five hundred years of empire.

More extensive walls were built around Rome and enlarged on many occasions. The great engineering work of the aqueducts and drains made the city livable and healthy for a population of over a million. As the brick gave way to more elegant stone, the city was graced with sculpture. There were thousands of statues, mostly copied from Greek models, in its porticoes and piazzas. Some of its temples were roofed with gilded tiles. The city flourished in magnificence for the next half millennium, largely on the momentum of its first three hundred years of empire. Many more of its emperors proved incapable of governing the city than the few who were successful. Reading the history of the emperors makes me wonder how it lasted as well as it did under such terrible mismanagement.

Edward Gibbon (1737–1794) is only the earliest (and probably the best) of the English authors to describe and probe the mystery of Rome's decline and fall. His best-known work is *The Decline and Fall of the Roman Empire*. Christopher Hibbert's *Rome: The Biography of a City* is probably the most manageable of more recent accounts. All the authors conclude that by the fifth century of the Christian era, there was little power left in the great city. Deserted by the emperor himself, preoccupied by an otherworldly Christianity, and overrun by Vandals and Arabs in the centuries following the relatively mild oppression of Alaric the Goth, it was left in the hands of a succession of popes, some spiritual leaders, some warriors, and not a few libertines. In the later Middle Ages the Roman population had shrunk from more than a million to a miserable remnant of less than twenty thousand people. Destruction of the aqueducts in the time of Genseric the Vandal had deprived the great centers of the imperial city of water. The remaining medieval population, reduced by disease and war, gravitated to the old Campus Martius area, close to the necessary water of the Tiber. Here were the remains of some of the early public works of the empire, the Pantheon, and the ruins of the circus of Emperor Domitian.

By the late Middle Ages, Rome had sunk to its smallest population, and the Campus Martius area contained the largest segment of the remaining population. The people pulled down the useless theater and recycled the cut stones of the circus seats to make more useful structures. But the shapes of the places of public amusement and the bloody spectacles of the gladiators' contests are still preserved in the buildings built from their pieces. A curved street between the Campo de' Fiori and the Corso Vittorio Emanuele II marks the location of the exterior wall of Pompey's theater, and the footprint of Domitian's circus contains the marvelous Piazza Navona, where *palazzi*, churches, houses, and restaurants surround elaborately sculptured fountains. The elongated oval is the heart of this area of downtown Rome. Two hundred and fifty meters to its south is the other, smaller open square, the Campo de' Fiori, a more plebeian but equally charming piazza that has became the center of our Roman experience. It contains all the essentials of a neighborhood: restaurants, bars, shops, a twenty-four-hour laundry, a flower market, several hotels, and a movie theater. Transportation to other parts of the city is close at hand. This is where we have chosen to be at home when in Rome.

The two piazzas present the two faces of the city. The Piazza Navona is sophisticated, prominent on the tourist agenda, expensive and charming. The Beautiful People are often here in chic costume and sunglasses. The Campo de' Fiori, on the other hand, begins each day as a public market, covered with irregular rows of the vegetable stands, fishmongers, and butchers, displays of kitchenware, hats, silk scarves, and both wholesale and retail flower merchants. Bent over and elderly, Italian women cut and wash vegetables at the bronze fountains that are supplied by the successors of the aqueducts of the Caesars and the Republic. These perpetually running water sources are marked with the ancient symbol, SPQR. According to some sources, this Latin inscription of SPQR (*Senatus Populusque Romanus*—the Roman Senate and People) was actually the abbreviation for *Sono porci questi Romani* ("They are pigs, these Romans.").[1] In the center of all this activity stands the forbidding statue of a severe scholar, Giordano Bruno, facing the rising sun, teaching by his presence many years after he was executed on this spot in 1600.

The Roman Inquisition of the fifteenth century and later was never as savage as that of Spain or southern France. Still, Bruno was surely a martyr to freedom of thought and inquiry. Galileo was imprisoned and abused, but not actually burnt for having taught truth to the world in a time when the Church rejected truth in favor of fundamentalist nonsense. Bruno was slightly more radical and closer to twentieth-century physics. He taught that our understanding of the world depended upon our location in space and time, and that there are thus an infinite number of ways of apprehending the reality of the

---

[1] The Roman water supply today is as lavish as it was under the empire. There are no reservoirs. A seemingly endless supply of good water runs into the city and out again into the Tiber. Fountains both functional and ornamental run day and night all through the year, governed by neither valve nor basin. There seems to be enough water up in the hills to let it flow perpetually.

universe. Although a Copernican, he insisted that it wasn't the only
way of explaining the motion of the stars and planets. Such relativism
got him in and out of various teaching jobs and made him almost as
unpopular with Protestants as with Catholics. The Venetian Inquisition
convicted him of heresy and shipped him to Rome where, after six
years in prison in the Castel Sant'Angelo, he was burned to death in
the middle of the Campo just four hundred years ago, a little more
than one hundred years before Isaac Newton showed us all how the
motions of the planets could be calculated from his direct and simple
laws of motion.

Recent though his immolation was, Bruno's statue was not put
up right away. It marks the place of his execution and that of a later
series of criminals and heretics throughout the seventeenth century.
After the establishment of the Kingdom of Italy in the mid-nineteenth
century, relations between the papacy and the government were
anything but civil. When a nobleman mayor of Rome expressed
jubilee greetings to the then Pope Leo XIII, Francesco Crispi, the
strongly anticlerical prime minister, fired the mayor and in 1887 put
up the statue of Bruno to make a clear statement about what he
thought of the current and past politics of the papacy. On the base of
the statue are likenesses and names of an extended group of "heretics,"
including Erasmus, Wycliffe, and Jan Hus, among others. Thus in the
Campo there is now an antipapal monument to freedom of thought.
It has long since ceased being a place of public execution. It does seem
odd that in such a civilized country, where Renaissance humanism
was born, there should have been the public execution of a thinker
for heresy within a generation of the date of the founding of Harvard
College. But then, Massachusetts was burning witches at an even later
date. We should never underestimate the power of reaction or the

danger of ideologues who wish to turn the world back to supposed primitive virtue by force of law, loyalty oaths, imprisonment, exile, book burning, and public execution.

This quarter of Rome, like all parts of the city, has a special history of its own. When you walk around a corner from the contemporary movie theater or fish market, you are likely to find yourself back in time by several centuries. Perhaps the lowest point in the history of Rome came at the end of the chaotic fourteenth century, when the Black Death reduced the already shrunken population by half. At this time French popes had spent almost a hundred years in "Babylonian Captivity" in Avignon. Prayers of saintly little Catherine of Siena were unable to convince Pope Urban V to stay in Rome for more than a visit. Urban VI did stay in Rome, but so divided the cardinals between Frenchmen and Italians that they elected at least two popes—sometimes three—at a time for forty years.

But some reconstruction of the city began during this time, around 1400. Houses were demolished and streets straightened. What happened to the owners or tenants of the homes thus destroyed doesn't seem to be recorded in any of the books I have read. Rent control hadn't been thought of as yet. Popes, and later on, dictators, undertook projects throughout the area of the old Campus Martius and its successor slums. Each new project involved tearing down whole neighborhoods and making way for the well-to-do to rebuild the quarter to their own taste and pleasure. Pope Julius II (Giuliano della Rovere), patron of Michelangelo and Raffaello, decreed the existence of the Via Julia at the end of the fifteenth century. The street, one block east of the Tiber, was laid out by Bramante at the pope's behest to make a better approach to the Vatican and the new Basilica of St. Peter that he was building. The private palaces that lined the Via Julia were the homes of the powerful families of sixteenth-century Rome. Today there are art galleries and jewelry stores along its attractive if shadowed route.

This is also the part of Rome that bore the brunt of the German and Burgundian savagery when Rome was sacked by the Protestants in 1527. To read the account of the late Renaissance scholar, Guicciardini, you might expect that there would be little left of Rome to restore. But within a decade, Pope Paul III (Alessandro Farnese) had embarked on three great projects: the repair of the city, the establishment of the doctrines of the Counter-Reformation of the Church, and the enrichment of his own family.[2] He presided over the foundation of the Jesuit order, the establishment of the Roman Inquisition, and the construction of the Palazzo Farnese. This huge building is set in the midst of the next square toward the river from the Campo de' Fiori. It is called the Piazza Farnese, a large, seemingly cold open space that contains the front of the huge palace with plenty of room to spare. While the building is severe, it supports an oversized projecting cornice that was designed by Michelangelo. The French acquired the palazzo a number of years ago and now use it as a symbol of their own grandeur, as their embassy to the Republic of Italy.

Looking to the towns to the north, Pope Paul III was also quite content to seize sizable domains to make duchies for his nephews or grandsons. But he also forbade the continuing dismantling of the Coliseum and other leftover classical buildings which were being used as quarries for the rebuilding of the city. Seeing the raw power of the occupants of the papal throne, implied by such building and city reconstruction, makes it hard to believe that papal "infallibility"

---

[2] His sister Giulia had been the wife of a member of the Orsini family, and at the same time the mistress of Paul's predecessor, Pope Alexander VI Borgia. I think the Via Julia may have been named in her memory.

is a much more recent doctrine, having been proclaimed by Pope Pius IX in the second half of the nineteenth century after Garibaldi had ended the personal rule of the Papal States.

On the northeast side of the Farnese square is the charming little church of the Brigittine nuns. In the early fourteenth century, while the popes reigned in Avignon and mobs ruled Rome, this quarter was a ruin of tumble-down houses, abandoned papal offices, and a miserable population of the poor. To live in a small house among them came a vision-inspired Swedish woman of distinguished family and obsessive charity, Brigitta Gudmarsson. She begged for the support of the needy and, like Catherine, interceded with the pope, Urban V, to return and take charge of the degraded capital. But the French pontiff found the decayed city too distasteful for long-term residence, and Rome remained in chaos for many more years. Still, Brigitta begged for help and dispensed blessing. She formed a community of nuns who are still there doing good works and singing the office in voices of such surpassing sweetness that visitors have said they define the sound of the celestial chorus in adoration.

Granting some allowance for the exaggeration inspired by finding such a congregation of women, both old and young, in the middle of the modern city, their gathering is an inspiration. Their only slightly modernized habits are gray with white trim on the coif and a pattern of golden tape on the simple headdress that suggests a crown; whether this is to show that they are brides of Christ or symbolic of their relationship to the old royal family of Sweden, I do not know. The headdress may also be related to the career of another Swedish immigrant, Queen Christina, who gave up her throne in her twenties, became a Catholic, and took up exile in Rome. She dressed rather like a man, charmed the Duc de Guise, spoke eight languages (including French, with an accent that even the French admired), and was a social success beyond imagining at the papal court of Alexander VII in the late seventeenth century.

At the southeast end of the Campo de' Fiori, the piazza gives way to a number of curving and intersecting little streets that seem to hide behind the Church of Sant'Andrea delle Valle and the Via dei Chiavari. Here in close proximity are located a number of middle-priced and, for Rome, economical hotels such as the Smeraldo, the Hotel In Parione (www.inparione.com), the Hotel Sole, and the Albergo della Lunetta, as well as our own, the Albergo Teatro di Pompeo. Restaurants abound, because the entire Campo is cleared of its markets, washed down, and relieved of its litter every day by noon. By then only the flower market in the northwest end remains, an attractive reminder of the morning's mercantile activity. The rest of the space is soon ringed with outdoor tables and chairs of establishments offering food and drink in all seasons. We once lingered late at an outdoor bar and then asked the proprietor if he could provide us with an early supper. He assured us that it would be his pleasure to do so, and in a few minutes called us in to an almost invisible dining room that had just six indoor tables. His menu was simple, but the gnocchi with Gorgonzola were delicious, the salad full of fresh tomatoes, and the *cantucci* replete with fresh almonds. It was one of the least-expensive dinners we ever found in Rome, and among the best.

Off the northeast corner of the Campo, diagonally across from the Albergo del Sole, is the Pollarolo, one of the great restaurant bargains of downtown Rome. Here we have dined exquisitely on several occasions for around $20 each, with a carafe of their good house wine.

There is a pleasant little coffee bar off the Via dei Chiavari and the Via dei Giubbonari, where we have sometimes breakfasted or met friends for a drink. Rosanna, the lady of the establishment

quickly adopted us when I asked for some munchies in preparation
for our friends' arrival.

"*Ah si, signore, capisco*," she said, nodding agreement, "*a Roma,
questa bar è il tuo salone*," obviously pleased that we had made her bar
our living room for our time in Rome. The good lady was also kind
to the unfortunate. Two mentally ill men seemed to stop in every
day for a coffee, on the house. One of them acted like an agitated
schizophrenic and was costumed in tight pink pants, a red shirt, and a
light-blue baseball cap. He greeted everyone with a loud and cheerful
series of non sequiturs. The other was less flamboyant and seemed
exhausted and burnt out. She gave them coffee. In every place we
visited in Italy, people seemed quite tolerant of unfortunates who
would be ejected from most restaurants in the United States.

This small neighborhood rapidly became so familiar to us that
going outside it added to the sense of adventure of being in a foreign
and exotic land. The sunken square of Largo di Torre Argentina is a
green island in the middle of the busy city where remains of Roman
buildings sprout up toward the sidewalk level and provide a haven for
a sizable population of cats that are either tolerated or encouraged
as municipal pets. This archaeological dig in the center of a great
modern city has revealed the remains of four small temples in the
neighborhood of Pompey's theater. It was in this portico of that public
building, next to a room where the senators met, that Julius Caesar
was murdered in 44 BC.

At the surface level here in a corner of the modern square is
one of the rare cab ranks in Rome. In most locations you have to
telephone for a cab, as none of them cruise for fares. And alongside
the Piazza Dell'Torre Argentina is the terminal of the tram line that
takes you across the river to Trastevere.

Walking due north from the Argentina took us to the Pantheon, the almost miraculously preserved Roman temple to all the gods, taken over by the Church in the seventh century. One of the misty figures of the Dark Ages is the Byzantine emperor, Phocas, who came to imperial power in AD 602 by leading a rebellion of the troops guarding the Danube. He is described as untutored, cruel, and utterly incompetent. But he gave the Pantheon to Pope Boniface IV and thus insured its preservation to our own time. Boniface rededicated it to St. Mary and All the Saints and Martyrs. Today it is also the burial place of the Savoyard kings of united Italy, as well as of the painter Raphael and a few others. The building is getting close to two thousand years old, having been built early in the second century by Marcus Agrippa and remodeled by Hadrian, whose inscription on the pediment still credits Agrippa for starting it all. It is an immense space, enclosed by a dome of a larger span than that of St. Peter's Basilica. The hole in the very center of the dome, called an oculus, was never filled in, and was designed to provide daylight. Evidently the updraft of natural ventilation in the huge space blows through it with sufficient consistency to keep much rain or many birds from coming in. How the concrete dome was cast is still pretty much a mystery today, but the Romans were the inventors of concrete and became masters of its potential.

We were awed but slightly chilled by the Pantheon. It seems a degraded sacred space that is now mostly an engineering marvel on the tourist itinerary. Its size and age are immensely impressive, but although massive, it provides about as much spiritual meaning as Grant's Tomb in New York.

The Piazza Navona is a couple of blocks east of the Pantheon. The shape of Domitian's circus is not immediately apparent to modern eyes; you only notice that there is a great area between two long rows of buildings with its ends closed in by constructions that

The Roman Pantheon

do little to suggest ancient Rome. But the curbstone defining its center seems to require us to walk around in the trace of ancient chariot races. When the circus was new, it was at least occasionally filled with water, and was the scene of gladiatorial naval battles. Today it is a sun-filled piazza of great size bordered on its outside by another unending series of restaurants and coffee shops whose proprietors set out bright yellow and white tablecloths and umbrellas on the sunny side of the square and take them in when the day progresses and the shadows change. There are simple pizzerias and gelato stands as well as upscale places to eat.

And in the center of the Piazza there are always people, most of them young and usually intent on enjoying each other. Few seem involved in earning a living except for the half-dozen itinerant artists who are doing portrait sketches of the tourists or vending derivative pastel paintings of the Roman scene. A few gypsy beggars sit disconsolately on the steps of the Church of St. Agnes in Agony. It is a lovely church despite its ominous name. Borromini designed it to stand in the traditional location where Agnes was martyred in the time of Diocletian. She was one of those lovely maidens of the early fourth century who dedicated their virginity to Christ at the age of twelve. Why the persecuting Roman authorities then forced her into a brothel when she was not yet of the age for a legal marriage (which they believed in) is unclear. Although naked, her miraculously long hair protected her from the view of the johns in the house, save one, who was struck blind when he tried to rape her. Agnes prayed for him and his sight was restored. Soon thereafter her breasts were cut off and she was beheaded. This took place in 314, shortly before Constantine decreed toleration of Christianity. It is the perpetual paradox of modern Italy that the symbols of young innocent chastity seem often to be displayed in conjunction with the *minigonne* and deep *scollatura* or loosely open suit jackets from the latest styles of the chic fashion houses of Milano and Turino. Italians are everlastingly in awe of female beauty, either of sanctity or sexiness. This admiration is not limited to men. And this is the country, after all, that made Sophia Loren an ambassador of the Republic and gave her a well-deserved knighthood.

Among the most marvelous ornaments of the Piazza Navona are the copy of an Egyptian obelisk in the center and the three ornamental fountains. Our favorite in all of Rome is Bernini's allegory of the four great rivers as they were known in the seventeenth century: the Nile, the Danube, the Ganges, and the River Plate. What might he have done if he had known about the Mississippi, the Amazon, the Volga, and the Huang Ho? Still, the work is as exciting a piece of sculpture as he ever carved. At the other end of the Piazza is his Fountain of the Moor, a figure he actually carved himself. The river gods are thought to have been done by assistants following his designs.

The Piazza Navona changed only gradually from a circus to a less-ferocious public gathering spot over the centuries. It became a marketplace in the late Middle Ages, and was paved in the fifteenth century when more of the rebuilding of Rome was begun under the pleasant papacy of Innocent VIII, the first pope to publicly recognize the parentage of his own children or to dine publicly with ladies. A century and a half later, Pope Innocent X, the founder of the Doria-Pamphilj fortunes, undertook further reconstruction of the square in the mid-seventeenth century. His first family palazzo here was modest when compared to the one built later, just a half-dozen blocks to the east. Today the architecture of the Piazza is a mixture of styles of many centuries, all of which seem to live together in happy harmony. Even the lighted signs over the local bank and several restaurants give a cheerful and homely quality to the place. No trip to Rome is complete without a sunny morning coffee or a late afternoon *aperitivo* in this perfect spot.

Once while we were living high by staying at the Albergo Teatro di Pompeo, we were directed by Luigi, then the voluble manager of the hotel, to visit the Palazzo Altemps. We had never heard of it, but Luigi was firm; we simply must go. I have learned to accede to this sort of insistence, and we went. One of the most recently commissioned museums in Rome, it was then only a year since it had opened, just two blocks beyond the north end of the Piazza Navona. The origin of the building goes back to the fifteenth century, but it was really put in shape by the family of Cardinal Marco Sittico Altemps, who arranged it for his collection of Roman sculpture in 1568.

Altemps was born in Austria, but was the nephew of Pius IV and had a right to the surname Medici. This was the period when popes and cardinals plunged enthusiastically into the excavation of the lost art treasurers of the previous thousand years. The palazzo was worked on by three or four of the great architects of the period, Sangallo and Martino Longhi among them. It seems that the Altemps family gave the building to the pope around 1900, and it eventually became the Spanish Seminary during the reign of Franco. The government of Italy bought it from the Vatican in 1982, and spent fifteen years restoring it as a museum of classical antiquities. The collection includes a marvelous assortment of Roman statuary, some of which was actually dug up by the original Cardinal Altemps.

The building surrounds a generous courtyard with first-floor loggia, from which we could see the sunny display of ancient statuary. Inside, many more figures and busts are displayed in a series of cool and elegant interconnecting rooms that allowed plenty of space for us to walk around and in between them. In the habit of artistic conservation of a few centuries ago, repairs to damaged parts of the works of art were carried out with great skill to make each piece look whole, with even the smallest cracks repaired with skillfully colored sealing wax. One statue had its missing foot restored by no less a master than Gian Lorenzo Bernini. I don't know what I think about this repair work. It makes sculpture from almost two thousand years ago look so clean that it is breathtaking. But it also makes our modern eyes register them as fakes even when they are 90 percent authentic. The whole problem is brought about by the fanatic Christians who went about knocking heads, arms, and penises off the statues of the gods to be sure that there was no idolatry going on around here. But, restored or not, the Altemps is a wonderful place for a leisurely visit. Fifteen pieces of the cardinal's own collection are here, together with a lavish collection of other Roman marbles.[3]

Between the two public squares of our home neighborhood runs the Corso Vittorio Emanuele II, a more contemporary street

---

[3] There are about a hundred marbles of the cardinal's original collection scattered around the world and in the museums of the Vatican, the Louvre, and the Hermitage. Works of art served as mediums of exchange during the eighteenth and nineteenth centuries. There may even be a few pieces of Altemps sculpture in the Metropolitan in New York.

of fascinating shops and public buildings. This *corso* is also the route of the famous Bus Number 64, the rapid and direct route from the railroad *termini* to the Vatican and St. Peter's. These buses are always crowded with jostling travelers, and the pickpockets on this route are the stuff of legend. If you take this convenient form of transportation across Rome, be sure to have your important papers secured, or perhaps even better, in the *cassaforte* at the desk of your hotel. But don't be timid about using public transportation; just be aware and take precautions. Thousands of Romans traverse these crowded buses daily, many of them elderly ladies with handbags. They simply clutch their purses to their bosoms and travel undisturbed.

Among other sites worth visiting on this grand avenue is the church of Sant'Andrea delle Valle, one of the purest and largest of the Baroque churches of Rome. The nave is lofty, full of light and, although swarming with statuary and painting, somehow seems free of the clutter of other buildings of the period. The church of Santa Maria Sopra Minerva is at the other end of the street. "Mary over Athena" presents the special interest of a Catholic church built on top of a Roman temple. Here Catherine of Siena, patron saint of all Italy, is buried, except for her head which was claimed by her hometown as an object of veneration. James Boswell witnessed a papal blessing here shortly before he set out to meet with his nightly amorous appointment.[4] It is a startling thirteenth-century Gothic building, the only one originally of such style in Rome. I guess the early Gothic age found Rome over-equipped with churches of earlier styles. This one is a pleasant anomaly of design and contains some wonderful features from later centuries, notably Michelangelo's

---

[4] Boswell recorded in his journal that his usual promiscuous behavior was surely permissible in Rome, where the better prostitutes were licensed by the Cardinal Vicar Apostolic.

statue of Christ holding the cross. This sculpture caused a scandal because of its nudity when it arrived from Florence in 1521. A gilded loincloth was added later on.

A block north of the Corso Vittorio Emanuele II, where the Via del Plebiscito and the Piazza Venezia connect, is the Palazzo Doria-Pamphilj, another of the more recently opened galleries that so ornament Rome in a time when even the aristocrats court the tourists. The building is vast and is divided into galleries and the family apartments, both of which can be visited by paying separate fees. We found that the admission charge of 8 euro also entitled us to a high-tech "acoustiguide" that responded to coded commands pressed into its keyboard each time we came to a work of art that had a bull's-eye symbol and an identifying number. The explanations recorded on the hundred or more taped segments were available in any of a half-dozen languages.

The English commentary was especially charming because it had been recorded by Jonathan Doria-Pamphilj, currently in charge of his family's affairs. All the Doria-Pamphilj family members trace their ancestry back to the nepotistic preferment arranged by the founder of the tribe, Pope Innocent X, who held the papal chair from 1644 to 1655, and who condemned the moralistic excesses of Catholic puritanism (Jansenism). Innocent had himself sculpted in a spectacular bust by Bernini and painted in an even more wonderful portrait by Velasquez. Both likenesses are in their own special room, *il gabinetto d'honore*, where they have been placed to make possible the comparison of the two artists' work. But other than this displacement, virtually all of the items in this enormous collection are hanging where members of the family placed them over the past three hundred years. There are paintings by Titian, Caravaggio, and Poussin, and a huge representation of all the artists up to the middle of the nineteenth century. Ten generations of this family have collected these works, while also playing the role of patron to musicians as well. Handel composed his first oratorio while living with the family. Arcangelo Corelli and Domenico Scarlatti found similar patronage. The musical instruments played by these great composers are still standing in a musician's alcove off the formal reception rooms. They look as though the musicians just went out for a cup of espresso and will be back to complete the concert in a moment.

One of the Pamphilj princes married an English girl in the early nineteenth century. She was probably rich and surely a beauty. The children have received at least part of their education in England ever since. As a result, Jonathan Doria-Pamphilj speaks fluent idiomatic English with just a trace of continental charm in the recorded commentary about the house. He tells the story of growing up in the enormous building where the baked clay tiles of the floors were rubbed with beeswax from the family farms to make them shine. The boy and his sister, he says, were often in trouble for roller skating around the elegant rooms and marking the *pavimento*. We nearly wore ourselves out in the long afternoon that we spent in the great gallery, and reflected that wheels on our feet might have been a good idea. The palazzo, opened in 1997, is recent among the public sights of Rome. It is worth the journey among the attractions of the Eternal City.

In this old downtown quarter there are also smaller and slightly less spectacular *palazzi* that repay a visit. One is the Palazzo Spada on the Piazza Capodiferro. It is located just southwest of the Piazza Farnese. In spite of the fact that the name and address translate as "Sword Palace at Iron Head Place," the Spada is a far-from-forbidding building that contains a number of paintings collected by the descendants of the family of Cardinal Spada over the last four hundred years, some by

Titian, Guido Reni, and Caravaggio. It seems to me that either the cardinal's taste was faulty or his purse too light to acquire the best of these masters. The most remarkable thing in the collection is a piece of trompe l'oeil architecture in the garden. Here Borromini designed an arched colonnade which connects the courtyards and gives the illusion of stretching into an almost distant space. Actually, the construction narrows and tapers on a rising pavement toward a theoretical vanishing point, and the true depth of the construction is quite shallow. A young museum guard demonstrated it to us by stepping over the interdicting rope and walking in through the receding arches. As he moved a few feet forward, he seemed to grow alarmingly in height, until after three paces he appeared to be a giant standing under the final arch. Smiling down on us, he raised the palm of his hand and placed it on the curved ceiling which had looked to be fifteen feet high before he entered it.

Foot distance from the Campo de' Fiori also can include an excursion across the Tiber via the Ponte Sisto, and thence due south to the Piazza Santa Maria in Trastevere: St. Mary across the Tiber, that is. This delightful square is a stopping point either before or after visiting the ancient church, reputedly one of the oldest in Rome. It seems hard to believe that this building was started by Pope Calixtus around AD 250, while Rome was still pagan. Its first form was completed by Julius I in the mid-fourth century. Various reconstructions took place in the twelfth century when Pope Innocent II commissioned a total reconstruction of the nave and crossing. An odd number of huge columns were liberated from the then disused Baths of Caracalla, and moved across the vacant ruined spaces of southern Rome to the river and thence to the site of the church. I presume they used oxen, wainropes, huge rollers, and barges to work the great monoliths several miles from the other side of the

Tiber. There are ten columns on the right side of the nave, eleven on the left. Two more even larger columns support the triumphal arch that frames the semicircular apse and the brilliant golden half dome behind the altar and its ciborium. This curved background is covered in gem-like mosaic, parts of it done in the twelfth century even though it was much reconstructed in the nineteenth.

This church is one of the most beautiful of this medieval quarter of Rome. Its piazza is a pleasant place for a coffee or an *aranciata* at one of the awning-sheltered tables in the square. While we were contemplating the sunny space, a little gypsy girl came begging to our table. We were conditioned to keep our distance from such kids, having once been the target of an unsuccessful pickpocketing by a group of preteen girls near the Coliseum a few years earlier. The waiter took a different tack. He gave the child a couple of small coins and told her to go away. The Italian attitude toward neighbors seems like something we might all learn from.

Just to the west of the river, a few blocks' walk from the Campo de' Fiori, is the old Jewish quarter of Rome where Pope Paul IV confined Roman Jews around 1558. He disqualified them from some occupations and from all honorable positions and seems to have invented—or at least introduced—the required yellow badge reinstated by the Nazis in the 1930s. He was not only down on Jews, but was also equally bloody-minded about other aspects of city and church authority. He published the first index of forbidden books, excommunicated (somewhat superfluously) Queen Elizabeth of England, and either destroyed or removed most of the "pagan" statuary from the courts and gardens of the Vatican. He condemned all sorts of sexual deviation or experimentation, and decreed that homosexuals should be burnt alive. With such broadminded spiritual direction as his, it is surprising that the Roman population got on with their Jewish neighbors as well as they did for the next four hundred years.

Actually, when this Pope Paul died, a delighted Roman population knocked the head off his statue, dragged it through the streets, and flung it into the Tiber. The crowd then turned to the Dominican monastery, the home of the order that staffed the Inquisition, and attempted to sack it. Many of the Counter-Reformation excesses of Paul's pontificate were not expurgated from "official" church regulation until the Second Vatican Council in the 1950s. Some groups within the church are trying to reinstate them even now.

One happy circumstance of this geographical concentration of Jews has been the existence of several very good restaurants with great breadth of cuisine at modest price and pleasant atmosphere. Al Pompiere is on the second floor (by American numbering) at Via Santa Maria dei Calderari 38. Roman friends took us there as though they were sharing a secret discovery.

Another very successful finding was the restaurant L'Eau Vive which, despite its name, is not particularly French in cooking or style. Located a few blocks north of the Corso Vittorio Emanuele II on Via Monterone, this restaurant is run by an order of Carmelite nuns who use the income from their cooking and serving to fund a number of charitable enterprises which they manage in Rome and in other countries. Dressed in various national costumes that range from corduroy jumper to silk sari, these dignified women take orders and serve beautifully prepared dinners in a simple dining room. The house wines are excellent. Finally, later in the evening when the guests have been served, the nuns gather at the side of the dining room and sing their prayer office of the day. It is a sort of spiritual floor show.

Out beyond our chosen neighborhood in the Roman "downtown," we have progressed to visit the Spanish Steps where John Keats shared digs with Shelley. The steps rise up in seemingly unending cascades to the church of Trinita dei Monte. The less-steep ascent from the south is along the Via Sistina, where we were once hustled by a plausible restaurateur and paid too much for an inferior dinner. The area is full of tourist traps whose sign is usually a foldout menu in four languages. But down at the bottom of the famous, flower-covered steps is the equally famous Caffè Greco, where Goethe took his coffee. The red plush chairs and the frock-coated waiters have changed little in the last century and a half, and if the drinks are on the expensive side, they seemed worth it to us. Once on our way back to the area of the Campo de' Fiori, we managed to stumble on the Fontana di Trevi in the eerie darkness. Its blue-green underwater lights made the riot of marble figures look like a classical ballet. We dutifully tossed our coins into the fountain to ensure our return to Rome in the future, and proceeded on our way to the little hotel near the Campo de' Fiori.

The Roman Forum and the Coliseum are worth an afternoon of anyone's first visit to Rome. The catacombs are also interesting, but over-advertised as the hiding places of persecuted Christians. They seem to have served as burial sites for all sorts of Romans for many years. The designation of the graves of the martyrs was largely a commercial project in the years when the trade in Christian relics was one of the most profitable businesses in Europe. There does seem to be some recent archaeological evidence that the bones of St. Peter do actually rest under the high altar at St. Peter's. The great basilica surely deserves a leisurely visit, as does the huge papal collection of works of art. The entire Vatican, of course, has to be visited and experienced.

The Galleria Borghese with its great sculptures by Bernini is surely a must-see, if only to see Canova's statue of Paolina, the sister of Napoleon, looking quite regal seated on her couch despite her almost complete absence of clothing. This perfect little museum is so small that reservations must be made by telephone.

Gian Lorenzo Bernini is the ultimate Roman artist, and surely the artist of papal Rome, while Michelangelo speaks for all the world. As we can see it today, the Basilica of Saint Peter is Bernini's work. Michelangelo's dome is nearly invisible from the Bernini Piazza around the obelisk, and his frescos in the Sistine Chapel are not visible to Romans at all—only to tourists who spend a few minutes viewing them as they speed along their tour. But Bernini's serpentine columns supporting the *baldacchino* are there for all to see in the church as well as in the newspaper photographs of the pope saying his prayers. Bernini's enormous sunburst, which is the focus of attention at the far end of the huge apse, is the ultimate baroque icon glorifying the Chair of Peter, the symbol of the power of the papacy. This center of theological and political force is made explicit by the explosion of baroque *putti* who radiate from the dove of the Holy Spirit that floats over the pope's empty chair, that rises even higher than the very altar where he celebrates Mass. Nowhere else is it more clear that Rome is about power.

Bernini, who lived in the baroque fullness of the seventeenth century,[5] was the most brilliant sculptor of his age, as well as the most Roman. He modeled himself as a damned soul and carved the result in marble. Bernini's head and shoulders show anger, force, perhaps even insanity, but the expression lacks the abysmal hopelessness of Michaelangelo's despairing soul staring out from the Last Judgment, clearly caught in the final stupefying knowledge of his sure and irretrievable damnation for all ages to come.

---

[5] He was a contemporary of John Milton and about thirty years older than Galileo. Spiritually and intellectually, he seems much closer to the latter than the former.

BERNINI as a DAMNED SOUL
c.1619

Here in the Borghese palace garden, you can see Bernini's amazing rendering of Apollo looking quite startled at the fact that Daphne is in the process of turning into a tree as he tries to get his hands on her lovely form. Persefone is being picked up by Pluto on the slopes of Enna in Sicily. The lecherous brute carries the distressed maiden aloft while his fingers squeeze into the flesh of her belly and buttocks in a tour de force of marble carving. There are Bernini statues all over Rome, but the best of them are these which he created on commission for Cardinal Scipione Borghese when the sculptor was just twenty-one years old, around 1620. It is hard to imagine a more divergent view of the world from that of the Puritans who were just then departing for Massachusetts in the *Mayflower*. No wonder early Massachusetts considered Rome to be the Whore of Babylon.

Other sites not to be missed include the exterior of the Colosseum and religious monuments like St. John Lateran, Santa Maria Maggiore, and the wonderful San Clemente, with its layer cake of architectural styles and spiritual traditions wrought from numerous rebuildings—a palimpsest of brick and marble which should be visited. Even our favorite small quarter of Rome is full of surprises and famous landmarks alike. It gives opportunities for tourist exploration to keep travelers busy for many weeks. The weedy and often nearly deserted Forum is a lovely walk. The Arch of Titus is there and has lasted well over the ages. It is a tradition that Jews should not walk under the arch which displays representations of the trophies brought back from Jerusalem by the boastful army of Titus that sacked it in AD 70. But learned Jews of my acquaintance have urged me to inspect it closely and admitted that they have done so too.

We have left Rome with regret each time we have headed for home, usually remembering to toss a coin into the bubbling waters of the Fontana di Trevi to ensure our return. From the Campo de' Fiori to Fiumicino Aeroporto Roma via cab is approximately 40 euro, about the same as a return to Manhattan from JFK in New York. But passing the church of Saint Paul's Outside the Walls along the way gives me the feeling that I have traversed a somewhat greater distance in both space and time between the hotel and the airport.

Perhaps one should not go to Rome on a first trip to Italy. It is essentially a different culture from the North, and it could be better assimilated after gaining some skill in negotiating the country and the language. Learn your way around Renaissance art first. For Rome was a backwater, and the pope was in France at Avignon during most of the years when the great artists shaped the new sensibility in the fourteenth and fifteenth centuries. Later, in the *quattrocento*, even strong popes like Martin V Colonna fled the city for years at a time and lived in Florence. Thus the artistic history of Rome largely skips from the classical period of the empire to the late Renaissance, mannerist, and baroque periods. Rome was nearly deserted during the Romanesque and the Gothic ages. The popes missed the cool purity of Piero della Francesca, the delicate simplicity of the Bellinis, and the disciplined inventiveness of Mantegna. Only later, with Raphael and Michelangelo, did Rome come into its own. Even then, Rome is a city consisting of architecture rather than painting. During the baroque age of Caravaggio and the later painters, connoisseur popes began to collect European art for their palaces in the Vatican. It is wonderful to see, but all this became more visible to us only after we had first explored extensively in northern Italy. After all, a first trip to Italy implies a preface to a second trip.

Still, lunching at a sidewalk café in the Piazza Navona and enjoying the waterfalls of Bernini's Fountain of the Four Rivers is a pleasant way to pass an afternoon. We may also have been unwitting extras in one of the movies that seem to use this relic of the Emperor Domitian's old stadium as a backdrop on an almost daily basis.

RESOURCES
Guidebooks and History Books

Do-it-yourself travel planning requires a certain amount of reading in advance. As in all agreeable human affairs, contemplation and anticipation add to the pleasure of consummation. We began with the budget guide put out by the Harvard Student Agencies, *Let's Go Italy*, an annually revised publication. In adding up the cost of the whole trip, guidebooks are small change. I would recommend that you try a couple of others as well. Our method was to choose the cheapest accommodations listed in the Cadogan travel guides (www.cadoganguides.com) or the most expensive from among the Harvard students' selections. We never went wrong sticking to this rule. Sometimes the dearest of the second book turned out to be listed as the bargain of the first, as was the case in Ferrara. Then our course was clear.

The hotels and *pensione* we stayed in ranged from adequate to splendid and cost from as little as $28 per night (in the late 1990s) to as much as $150 (in 2008), depending on the city and the extent of its popularity among tourists. We always had our own bathroom and usually lots of pillows, towels, and blankets, although I will admit that there is sometimes a cultural difference between the American and the Italian idea of a proper bath towel.

Although the guidebooks gave us a good skeletal outline of the principal artworks and how to find them, we also used the long, thin Michelin Green Guide. It is somewhat more inclusive of the monuments and the artworks, but its comments are telegraphic and sketchy. It also provides pretty and accurate little city maps with cabalistic legends that I have almost never been able to decode. Its odd shape requires a shoulder bag with a wide side pocket to slip it in crosswise, but this made it more portable than the other, fatter guidebooks. The *Green Guide* does not give information on survival arrangements for food and shelter that are detailed in incomprehensible codes in the Michelin Red Guide. Since restaurant ratings by means of stars and forks are meaningless in Italy, where the simplest *trattoria* may have perfectly wonderful food, we eliminated that one and eventually took to garnering local recommendations from the desk clerk or the owner of the *albergo* where we were staying. You get what you pay for in most Italian restaurants, and the menu is posted by law in the front window, a pretty reliable guide. I don't think we ever had anything but a good dinner on any of our trips, and we almost never experienced a snooty waiter in Italy.

The trouble with all the guidebooks, and there are a great number of them, is that no single volume gave us quite enough information, and each was short on the historical background and artistic history of what we were going to see. Our journeys were greatly enriched by doing quite a lot of very pleasant homework in history and art books ahead of time and between trips. If we didn't remember it all, much of it did come back to consciousness when we were confronted by the very stuff of Italy. By far the best book we found was H.V. Morton's *A Traveler in Italy,* last reprinted in the 1970s and now, sadly, out of print. We found our copy in a secondhand bookstore. Others may be as fortunate, or able to locate it in a library or online, using various websites that list rare and out-of-print books for sale (i.e., www.abebooks.com and www.alibris.com). Google and Wikipedia are essential additions to the home library. There are more or less understandable English-language guidebooks available at the tourist bureaus in most of the cities of the peninsula, but one must go there to buy them, so they are best brought back to be perused at home. Following this method, we collected books and pamphlets wherever we went and subsequently found our second trip to Venice much more rewarding than the first (although *any* trip to Venice is wonderful). Much later, also in another secondhand bookstore, I found Julia Cartwright's two-volume biography of Isabella d'Este and Raphael Sabatini's *Life of Cesare Borgia.* They bring the Renaissance alive with mixed joy and fury.

Contributing to this spate of travel literature, I have here tried to pass on some salient stuff about a few beautiful and even some terrifying locations from Rome, the Veneto, and Lombardia to Emilia-Romagna, Tuscany, and Umbria, as well as a few towns farther south. We found we enjoyed smaller cities and towns more than big ones. My own books, *About Italy: Puglia to the Po* and *About Sicily* might be useful in this regard.

Reading good books about Italy ahead of time helped get us into the proper frame of mind, just as reading Mark Twain before taking a boat down the Mississippi would, or Rachel Carson before walking the beaches of the Carolinas or the rocky shores of Maine. We are able to really see only what we know well enough to recognize when it is there, right under our eyes and noses. Things we didn't know about on our first visit, like the nonbarking dog in Sherlock Holmes's *Silver Blaze*, are likely to be invisible when our senses are occupied with many new impressions. There's hardly a bare brick wall in Siena or Milan that doesn't enclose some bloody tragedy or ecstatic vision, some poignant love story, mayhem, or artistic gesture.

On the other hand, we found much in Italy that is immediately apparent to anyone's eye. We used to think that the films of Fellini and the operas of Donizetti and Verdi were great feats of artistic invention. Even after spending our first few days in the country, we realized that the former had a genius for re-creating in front of the camera what goes on in all Italian markets, homes, piazzas, bedrooms, and churches, every day of the year. The two operatic composers merely gave a musical setting to what the Italians have felt about themselves and the meaning of love, honor, and parting since they began that long climb back from the collapse of the Roman Empire.

A great number of Americans who have the time to travel, think foreign lands are intimidating, especially those where not everyone speaks English. Thus, many select a group tour by bus. I am sure there is fun and even companionship to be found that way, but this book is an apologia for the self-guided tour and an attempt to convince friends that we need not take our adventures in such a regimented form. The fun of cruising around Italy on impulse should not belong exclusively to the college kids with rucksacks on their backs and packs on their fannies. We think that mature adults also will, in fact, have more fun finding their own way around Italy. It is, after all, a country which for centuries has been accustomed to tourists and is well set up to receive them. Most touristic services are controlled in price by governmental decree. Government ratings of hotels and *alberghi* are reliable. In the northern cities we visited, street crime is rare and service personnel are both helpful and honest. Taxi driving is much more of a dignified vocation in Italy than the temporary pastime of marginal characters or scoundrels that it can sometimes be in large American cities. None ever took us for a ride, even when we looked hopelessly confused. Several gave us excellent advice. One examined our costume and baggage and offered the opinion that we would not stay at the bargain-priced hotel we named for more than a one-night stand. He was right: It was the only really grubby hotel we experienced on any trip, and we should have followed his advice. He also pointed out an excellent little bar and café for lunch. Similarly, waiters in restaurants were reliable fountains of information about the towns we visited. The innate courtesy and politeness of Italians will come as a pleasant surprise to most big-city Americans. It may well be a shock to New Yorkers.

Piazzetta Castelvecchio, Arco di Gavi   VERONA

~Finis~

Some Suggestions for Further Reading

While this is not a bibliography of all that we have read about Italy, these titles are among the many interesting and useful books that we have read. Some are old and a few are out of print, but they are worth looking up in libraries, secondhand bookstores, or on the Internet.

Lives of the Most Excellent Painters, Sculptors and Architects, by Giorgio Vasari (Florence: 1550 and 1568) is a monumental work, which in some editions can run to as many as five volumes in Italian. There are, however, a number of good abridgments in English, such as that published in paperback by Viking Penguin, New York and London, 1988. Although sometimes criticized as being of variable accuracy, the biographies of artists of the Renaissance are quite wonderfully fresh, even today. Vasari's personal relationship with Michelangelo makes that essay especially interesting.

Wonderfully detailed histories can be found in Christopher Hibbert's books, *Florence: The Biography of a City*, and *Rome: The*

Biography of a City (New York: W.W. Norton, 1993). As well as recounting the scandals and gory incidents that are missing from other histories, these books are beautifully illustrated.

Alternating between humorous and doomsday views of the Italian character, *The Italians: A Full-Length Portrait Featuring Their Manners and Morals*, by Luigi Barzini (New York: Macmillan, 1977), which was originally published in 1964, makes some predictions that have not as yet come about. It includes an interesting and somewhat sympathetic history of the Sicilian Mafia.

A Traveller in Italy, by H. V. Morton (New York: Dodd, Mead, 1964) rambles on about everything from the partisan execution of Mussolini to the frescoes of Florence and the poison antidotes of ancient Rome. Morton is a most genial traveling companion in northern Italy. For a happy blend of history, travelers' tales, and sensitive descriptions of the great works of art, Morton is the best. It is a pity that this book has been allowed to go out of print, although it is available online (i.e., www.abebooks.com).

As you might imagine from its source, *Let's Go Italy*, published biennially by Let's Go Inc., a subsidiary of the Harvard University Student Agencies (New York: St. Martin's Press), this guidebook is written for the young of heart, soul, and body, as well as for those of a limited purse. Travelers of a more sedate age may find some of its recommendations for lodging primitive, but choosing the more expensive listed will provide a perfectly decent place to stay. Recommendations of what to see and how to find it are breezy, incisive, irreverent, and accurate.

We found the most useful of all guidebooks to be *Lonely Planet Italy*, published biennially, up-to-date with both fax and phone numbers, for 1,000 places to stay. We also found the Cadogan Guides to be very useful.

Long out of print, The *Life of Cesare Borgia, Duke of Valentinois and Romagna,* by Rafael Sabitini, is an entertaining biography that presents a persuasive defense of the lifestyle of the Borgias, including Pope Alexander VI. Sabatini defends the honor of the often-maligned Lucrezia against the ungallant criticisms of Victor Hugo.

Isabella d'Este, Marchioness of Mantua 1474–1539: A Study of the Renaissance, by Julia Cartwright (Mrs. Ady), 2 vols. (London: John Murray, 1904). There are probably more-recent editions of this great work, but finding the ancient original in a secondhand bookstore was a treat. The Victorian author skirts around some of the spicier incidents of the *quattrocento,* but her indefatigable research into the lives of her subjects and liberal quotation from Isabella's letters (almost all of which still exist) make this one of the most authentically flavorful accounts of the period. Popes, poets, scholars, courtiers, warriors, painters, emperors, and sculptors all knew and corresponded with *la prima donna del mundo.* Almost all of the great characters of the Italian Renaissance are to be met with here.

Today the Google search engine on your computer is probably the best to preselect places to land in Italy.

INDEX